Rameses III:Father of Ancient America

Jairazbhoy, R. A.

All Rights Reserved.
© 1992 Jairazbhoy, R. A.

No part of this publication may be reproduced, stored in a retrieval system, or transmitted in any form or by any means, electronic, mechanical, photocopying, recording, or otherwise, without the prior written permission of the copyright owner and/or the publisher.

First published in Britain and the USA
by Karnak House
300 Westbourne Park Road
London W11 1EH
England

British Library Cataloguing in Publication Data
Jairazbhoy, R. A.
Rameses III: Father of Ancient America
I. Title
932

ISBN 0-907015-73-5
ISBN 0-907015-88-3

RAMESES III

FATHER OF ANCIENT AMERICA

R. A. Jairazbhoy

Of all forms of innovation, cultural borrowing (which the historical anthropologist calls 'diffusion') is by far the most common and important. The overwhelming majority of elements in any culture are the result of borrowing. Modern American culture provides a good illustration, as can be shown by a few random examples. Our language comes from England, our alphabet from the Phoenicians, our numerical system from India, and paper and printing from China. Our family organisation and system of real property derive from medieval Europe. Our religion is a composite of elements largely assembled from the ancient Hebrews, Egyptians, Babylonians and Persians. Metal coinage comes from Lydia, paper money from China, checks from Persia. Our system of banking, credit, loans, discounts, mortgages, et cetera, is derived in its essentials from Babylonia, with modern elaborations from Italy and England. Our favourite flavours in ice creams — vanilla and chocolate — are both borrowed from the Aztecs of Mexico and were unknown to Europeans before the conquest by Cortez. Tea comes from China, coffee from Ethiopia, tobacco from the American Indians. Our domesticated animals and plants, virtually without exception, are borrowed. If the reader were to make a list of absolutely everything he eats during the next week, analysis would probably show that one third are products that were already cultivated in Neolithic times, and that it would be surprising if the list contained any item that was not cultivated for food somewhere in the world when Columbus sailed for America.

Our culture is not unique in this respect, for it is doubtful whether there is a single culture known to history or anthropology that has not owed at least ninety per cent of its constituent elements to cultural borrowings. ▌

George P. Murdoch
"How Culture Changes" in *Man, Culture and Society,* H. L. Shapiro, ed., OUP, New York, 1960, pp. 253 - 40.

CONTENTS

PROLOGUE

Columbus had sailed to what he thought was China, and in his wake the culture of the natives declined and disappeared. The Egyptians, on the other hand, sailed to what they thought was paradise, and they brought with them their knowledge and a higher form of life that took root. It was assimilated, and made into something so different that its mysteries are only just beginning to be unravelled.

And they changed the visual scene. Where there had been farms and small villages, there now grew great ceremonial centres with massive stone carvings and pyramids with temples. Now for the first time trade and industry flourished, arts and crafts became specialised, people learned the rudiments of writing and enjoyed spectacle sports; rituals and ceremonies were performed, gods with attributes were worshiped, ideas of the afterlife gave hope, a collective conscience grew, a hierarchy evolved with kings, priests, soldiers, commoners and slaves. Through journeying in the land, the cultural ideas spread, and through the strength of oral tradition they survived and became a permanent inheritance. So it is surely fair to say that this Egyptian voyage to Mexico, for which the evidence is set out here, was one of the most momentous voyages ever to have been undertaken to Mexico. The first chapter is restructured and summarised from the author's work published between 1974 and 1981 (for details see References). This account constitutes only one phase of the impact of the Old World on the New, though this phase was the most crucial because it was formative — that is, one in which high civilization first appeared in the Americas. From its settlements on the Gulf Coast the Egypto-Olmec culture made forays into the highlands of Mexico and, as I have shown elsewhere, a contingent of them migrated to South America and transmitted there powerful influences. It would have been surprising if they had not attempted to make inroads into the territories north of the Mexican Gulf. I shall endeavour to show in the second chapter that they did indeed do so. Moreover visible traces of contact between Mexico and south east United States continued into later periods, in some instances still bearing imprints of their common Egyptian source.

Chapter 1

PART 1

RAMESES III, FATHER OF OLMEC MEXICO

Figure 1

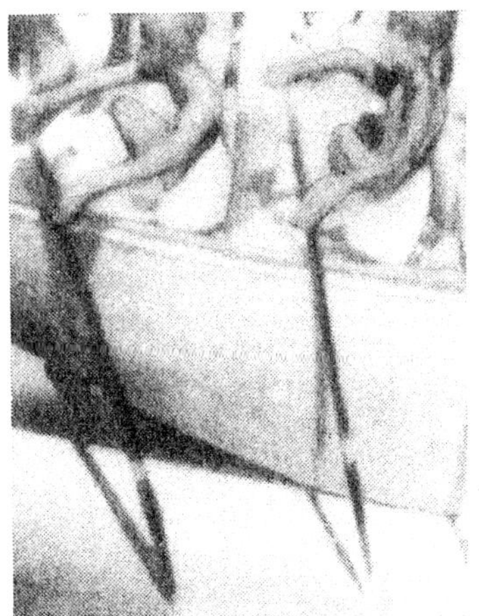

Figure 2

Mexico is a land of volcanoes. But there is one very special volcano, an extinct one, that lies in the heart of the Olmec lands near the south-west shores of the Gulf of Mexico. What is so special about San Martin Pajapan is that, apart from Easter Island, it is the only volcano in the world in whose crater a monumental sculpture has been found. It dates from about 1000 BC. Why should they have dragged it up a thickly wooded slope (even with modern equipment it was brought down with great difficulty), and put where no one is likely to have seen it? That is, except those who went up there to perform rituals, and to bury offerings underneath it?

Observe this figure (Fig.1) closely. He has a jaguar mask above his head, and he squats holding a bar with both hands. Notice the way he is sitting — he uses one foot as a cushion, while the other leg is folded back at the knee. This is a unique posture in the art of the entire ancient world, and mainly oarsmen in Egyptian boats sit in this manner (Fig.2). So he *could* be an oarsman. But why are the oars short? Either because of the difficulty of carving full length oars out of a single block of stone, or because they are merely symbolic.

His elaborate head-dress proves that he is no ordinary boatman — more likely a god or a king. I maintain that he is the Egyptian Pharaoh Rameses III, and more than that, it is Rameses sitting in his boat in Paradise (Fig.3), which is painted in his Temple in Thebes. This is proved by seven particulars that they share in common (Fig.4).

Both wear wrist and arm bands, and more importantly, a head cloth whose lappets fall over the ears onto the shoulders. It is called the *nemes* crown in Egypt, and is worn only by the Pharaoh. Again, only the Pharaoh could wear a uraeus on the brow, which is a fire-spitting serpent. The Mexican figure has serpents beside the brow, and they are actually flam-like. Finally, in addition to the posture, the oars, the items of apparel, and the snake diadem, both have three crosses over the head. In Egypt they are hieroglyphic signs for 'city', and imply here the heavenly city in the underworld. And similarly, in Mexico the cross-in-disk signifies the sun in the Underworld.

Figure 3

Figure 4

Why should Rameses have wanted a statue of himself sitting in a crater in the far west of the world? Because in Egyptian belief the sun entered the Underworld in the Far West, and the Pharaoh accompanied him on his ship. Rameses writes in his inscriptions that he has actually reached this mountain in the far west of the world [1] which was known as Manu. A statue of himself in it would be an insurance of resurrection there, just as servant statues were commonly put in Egyptian tombs to ensure that they would come alive to serve in the hereafter. Such a statue would no doubt have been present in the solar ship, since the *Book of the Dead* (ch. 130, 31 and rubric) directs that "thou shalt place a figure of the deceased in the bows of Ra's boat" and describes it as "sitting upon his thigh."

There were several reasons why I identify St. Martin on the Mexican Gulf with Manu — one, because it literally is as far west as you can sail from Egypt; two, because of the statue and its Egyptian affinities; three, because the Aztecs still preserved the conception of the place where the sun enters[2] (it was known as *ciuatlampa)*; and four, because of a visible resemblance between the real and the mythical mountain — both having twin peaks (Fig.5). Here one sees the solar ship approaching the twin-peaked mountain on Seti's sarcophagus (Fig. 6). [See Postscript.]

Of course when the migrants found that the sun did not literally set in the crater, they must have been beset with doubts. Some must have decided to go away and continue their search, as Mexican texts actually say,[3] and others stayed on and made the

Figure 5

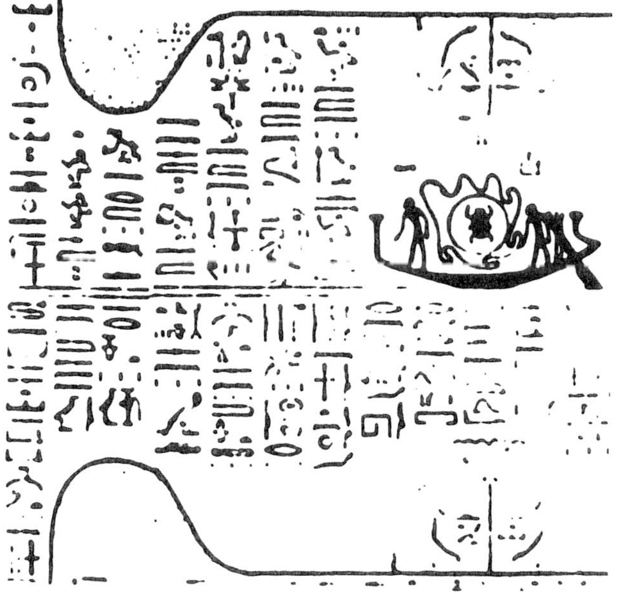

Figure 6

mountain the focus of a cult, which we know it was.

As for Rameses, his presence in Mexico is verifiable by yet another work — a painting recently found on a pyramid at Las Higueras in Vera Cruz state (Fig.7). Again its resemblance is with the same picture of Rameses III boating in the Underworld (Fig.8). So alike are they that the head and profile could go over one another and make an almost exact fit. Then too the winged disk over the head of the Mexican figure is matched by the winged disk (Fig. 9) over the picture of Rameses III in his solar ship. Only the lower part of the Mexican figure remains to be explained. His proportions suggest that he assumes this shape because he is sitting on his haunches. Such squatting statues were carried about by porters in

Figure 7

Figure 8

New Kingdom Egypt as seen in as seen in this wall painting from a tomb in Thebes (Fig. 9). Proof that the Mexican figure was such a statue, and was carried about by litter bearers, are the projections on the base which would have been intended for inserting

Figure 9

the parallel poles.

In Egypt there was an oracular god who was carried about in this manner. A text of Rameses XI says that it was on a pedestal carried about on poles.[4] It was addressed when it halted, and it replied by vigorously nodding its head. And there is remarkable confirmation that the Egyptians brought this god with them to Mexico. Sahagun records that the ancestors who had come from across the seas to Mexico brought with them an oracular god who was carried about on the backs, and this god went advising them.[5] Since I have shown that the oracular god of Las Higueras has the features of Rameses III, it is evident that the oracular god brought by the ancestors was the Pharaoh who sent the expedition. So in effect Rameses continued to go on advising and directing the migrants through his animated statue.

Figure 10

To add to the mobile figure of Rameses that was carried about, and the static one in the crater, the very name of Rameses III is preserved in Mexican tradition. Here is what the Epic of the Mayas, the *Popol Vuh* records.[6] It says that some of the descendants of the ancestor who had emigrated here, decided to return to the land of their fathers. They crossed over the sea to the sunrise, met Naxcit, the ruler of a large kingdom who gave them the regalia, including the canopy and throne, and they brought these back across the sea. Compare the name Naxcit with Nakht, which was part of Rameses III's Horus name (that is, one of the five names of the Pharaoh).

Again the fact that the regalia was brought back from Egypt is confirmed by its actual presence in Mexico. To add to the *nemes* head cloth and the uraeus snake which we have already seen, I have been able to identify the double crown, the feathered parasol, the flail, the tail, and one of the coronation

Figure 11 Figure 12

rituals.

Here they are: This Olmec bearded ruler on a stele wears a double crown (Fig.11) made up of a falcon with a serpent above. Compare the double crown of Egypt with the vulture and serpent in the same relative position on the Pharaoh's head (Fig. 12). They symbolise dominion over the north and south of the land.

The ceremonial parasol composed of concentric rings of feather mosaic occurs in the paintings of the same Las Higueras pyramid mentioned before (Fig.13). And here it is on the Temple of Rameses III at Madinat Habu (Fig. 14). Even the colour scheme is virtually the same, i.e., light blue/green, dark blue

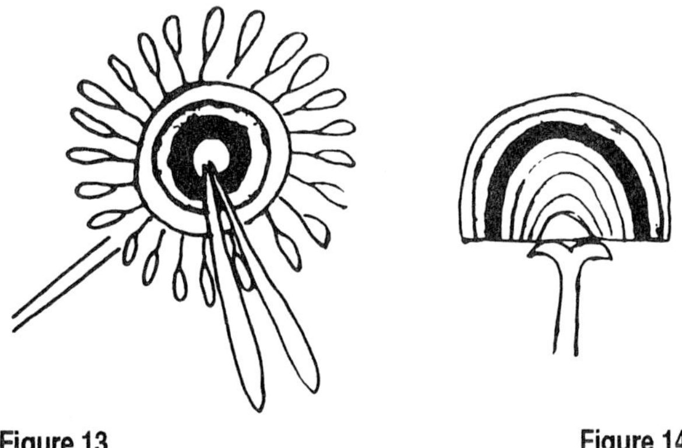

Figure 13 **Figure 14**

and red.

No other civilised ruler but the Pharaoh wore an animal tail as part of the royal dress (Fig. 15). And yet here it is in Mexico worn by the same Olmec king (Fig. 16) who has the double crown, and again it is attached in just the same place above the belt. Another give-away feature is that his head and feet are carved in profile while the chest is in full frontal; this is an exclusively Egyptian artistic convention.

The flail is to be seen here in this Olmec painting

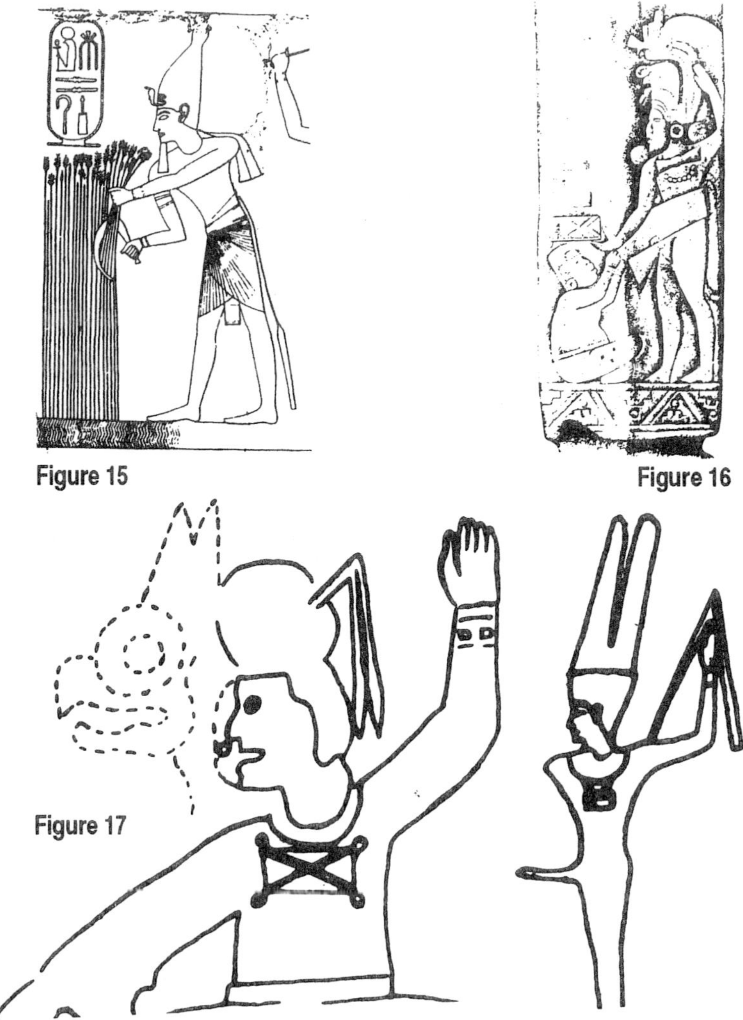

Figure 15

Figure 16

Figure 17

Figure 18

from the cave in Oxtotitlan (Fig.17). The figure lifts one arm just like the Egyptian god Min (Fig.18), who is actually called "god of the uplifted arm." Both have the flail hanging behind their head.

A Nahua poem describes a ritual in which by

shooting arrows to the four quarters a man becomes god. In the Egyptian Sed Festival arrows were shot to the four quarters before the king was proclaimed (and hence became a god).[7]

Another Maya document, the *Titulo Coyoi,* confirms that the regalia was brought by-the migrants: 'These things came from the East, from the other side of the water and the sea: they came here, they had their throne, their little benches and stools, they had their parasols and bone flutes...'[8]

This must refer back to Olmec times since we know that it was then that stools and altars were first used as thrones. More than just the regalia, the Egyptian migrants very likely introduced the very idea of kingship.

I shall now show that all the chief stages of Rameses III's life left a mark in Mexico and beyond. They include his birth, youth, marriage, conquest, death and afterlife.

BIRTH. A text describes the birth of Rameses as resulting from the creator god in his form as a ram co-habiting with his human mother.[9] This Olmec sculpture of a jaguar copulating with a woman (Fig. 19) must have the same meaning. This is suggested by the explanation given by native Indians of a similar ancient sculpture in Colombia — that the union of the woman and beast resulted in the birth of a hero.[10]

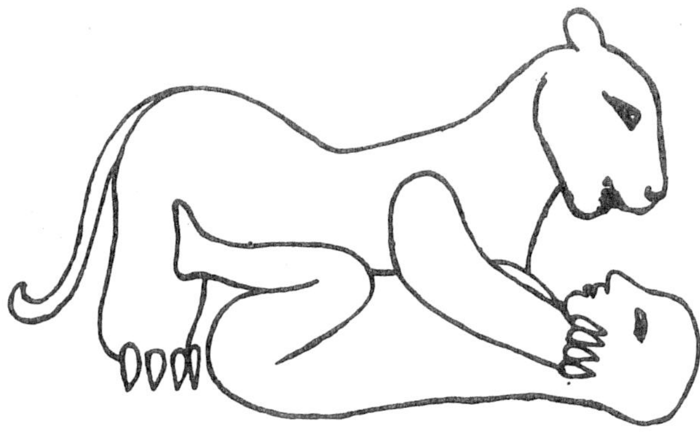

Figure 19

YOUTH. The distinguishing attribute of the royal Egyptian child was a sidelock; indeed the sidelock was actually the hieroglyph meaning "child". Compare this sidelock of Rameses II as a youth (Fig. 20) with this scroll on the head of a sculpture of a child in West Mexican art (Fig. 21). Again the

Figure 20

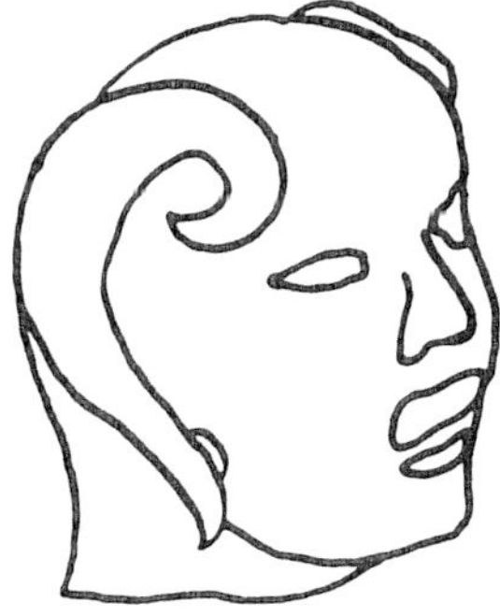

Figure 21

sidelock appearsfor the first time in Olmec Mexico.

Figure 22 Figure 23

MARRIAGE. It was customary in ancient Egypt for the king to marry his sister. This unique practice prevailed also in South America. In Peru the Inca king alone was allowed to marry his sister.[11] This is only one of many Egyptian ideas surviving in Peru.

CONQUEST. The Pharaoh conquering his enemies was a favourite theme in Egyptian art. Here is Rameses III in this role (Fig. 22). Almost every detail is identical in a Mexican picture book (Fig. 23). Both protagonists stride forward, raise their weapon to strike, and hold the enemy by his hair. The victim kneels and lifts one finger in token of surrender — a gesture exclusively of Middle Eastern origin.

Figure 24

The whole sequence of action is without parallel anywhere else.

Rameses makes much of his act in which he recounts how many thousand private parts of his enemies he had cut off,[12] seemingly to dissuade them from invading Egypt again.

This highly unusual treatment must have been meted out to the victims at Monte Alban. They are writhing minus their manhood from which blood is flowing (Fig. 24). The hieroglyphs by their side, some of the first in the Americas, are thought to name the captive tribes, and this too is exactly paralleled by the reliefs at Rameses' Temple.

DEATH. In Egypt alone the body was laid out with arms crossed over the chest. This is the mummy of

Rameses III (Fig. 25). And here is an Olmecoid statue from Western Mexico (Fig. 26); his exposed ribs indicate he is dead. Perhaps his bowels have been taken out and replaced with aromatic substances. While this was the usual practice in Egypt, it was also known in Mexico.[13] And another thing — Mexicans placed masks over the face of the dead (Fig. 27). This first began in Olmec times, and this Olmec jade mask (Fig 28) is reminiscent of an Egyptian one in wood (Fig 29).

Figure 25

Figure 26

AFTERLIFE. The afterlife of the Egyptians was a rural paradise called Yaru. Here Rameses III is seen ploughing and reaping its barley (Fig.30). It grows with exceptional vigour there, and its exact dimensions are given. The Mexicans also conceived the Underworld as the "house of corn", Cincalco. And again in Peruvian belief the land of the dead was noted for having "many fields."[14]

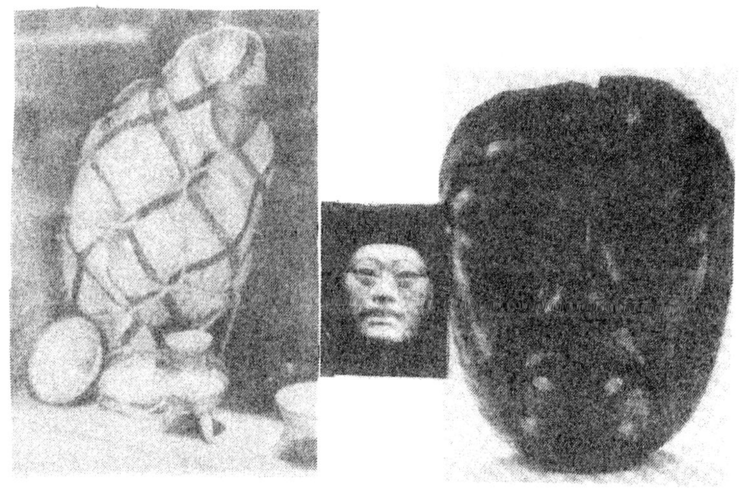

Figures (left to right): 27, 28, 29.

it is patterned after the Egyptian Yaru.

We have passed in review the portrait, the name, the royal insignia, and a whole sequence of stages in the career of Rameses III as manifested in Mexico and Peru. It remains now only to hear what he himself has to say relating to this matter.[15] On one occasion he says that he built warships, galleys and coasters on the Mediterranean and sent them to "the ends of the earth" to bring back goods to enrich the treasuries of Egyptian temples. On another occasion he says he built great galleys and sent them "into the sea of the inverted water," including some to the land of Punt (down the Somali coast) which returned safely with goods. If

Figure 30

others did not come back they would not have been mentioned, since Egyptian kings never publicised their reverses. But there was never any doubt that they had reached the ends of the earth — Rameses IV declares that "the Ocean and the Great Circuit ... to the ends of the supports of the sky" were under his father's grasp.[16]

No doubt in sending an expedition to the West, Rameses would have had in mind a dual purpose. A celestial journey to the West of the World was his rightful expectation as Pharaoh. Ever since the Old Kingdom the Pharaoh had been described as sitting in a boat, taking the helm, and being rowed to the West over the two parts of heaven.[17] Rameses is represented in this role (Fig.31) in one of the rooms in his tomb in Thebes, and the text there is 'The Litany of the Sun," proving that it was the solar journey that was intended. Before they had deteriorated, the paintings were reproduced

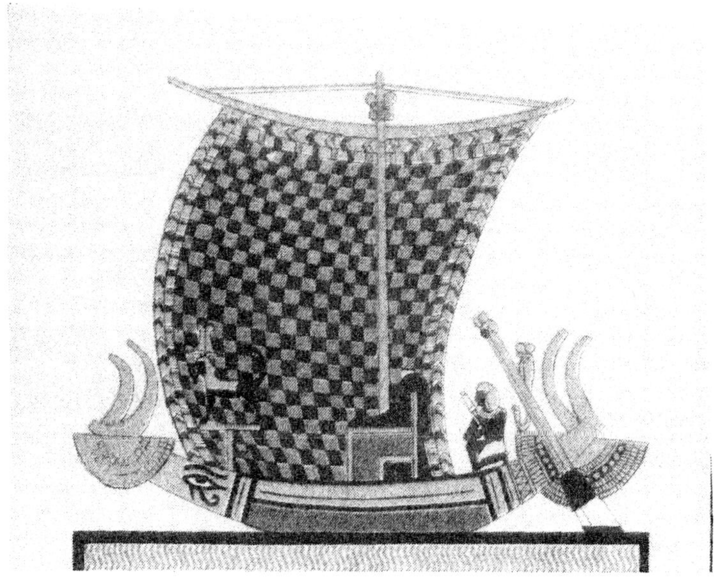

Figure 31

and it is clear that there was a fleet of seven ships.[18] It is highly unlikely that the fleet that Rameses says he sent to the ends of the earth and to the sea of the inverted water, would have been unconscious that the entrance to the Underworld lay in the Far West of the World; and so it could be said that they actually came looking for the Underworld. And this is exactly confirmed by the Mexican tradition preserved by Sahagun in which the first settlers of this land are described as coming in seven wooden ships or galleys, and they "come looking for a terrestrial paradise."[19] The many Mexican conceptions of paradise and the whole solar cycle that are both patterned on the Egyptian, as we shall see, proves motives.

There is yet another indication that the voyagers were impelled by religious motives, and were being guided by religious texts. The *Popol Vuh* relates that the ancestors who came from the sunrise were called 'Branches'.[20] In the Egyptian *Book of What is in the Underworld* one of the boats journeying through the Underworld is called 'the Branch' (Fig.32). So it is likely that the crew of the boat named 'the Branch' called themselves Branches since they were emulating the solar voyage. A solar emblem from the prow of the sun's ship survives in later Mexico. It is the Horus prow (here from the Ramesseum in Thebes (Fig.33), and just as in the prow of the Maya boat (Fig.34), the falcon head has a garland of lotus leaves which rules out any question of coincidence.

Figure 32

The chief claim to fame of Rameses III had been his conquest of the Sea Peoples. His Temple walls at Madinat Habu depict the naval battle, the first such pictured monumentally. If Egypt had fallen then to the combined Mediterranean powers its history might

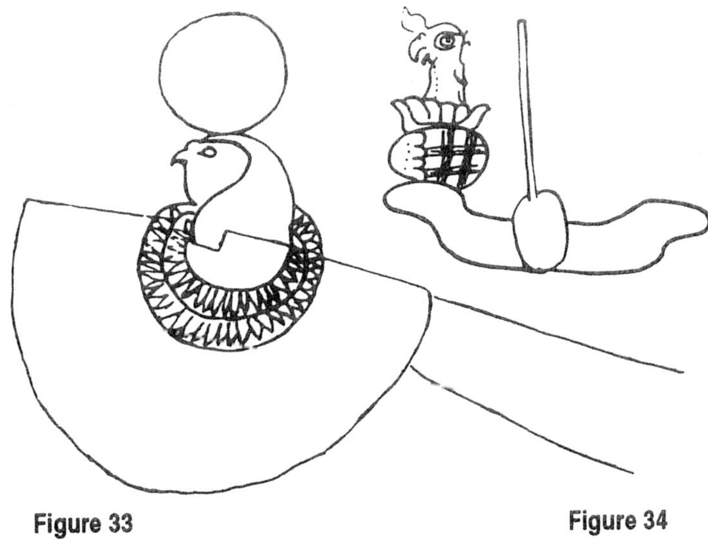

Figure 33 **Figure 34**

have been very different. But again had he not sent the expedition to the far west of the world, the transformation of Mesoamerica would not have come about, and taken the turn that it did. When stock is taken of the achievements of the Pharaohs, Rameses III will have to be accorded the double distinction — *saviour* of Egypt and *father* of Olmec Mexico.

PART II

VOYAGERS FROM THE OTHER SIDE OF THE OCEAN

The next question relates to the personnel — who were the expeditionary members, and what are the proofs of their presence?

The repeated occurrence of identifiable Egyptian deities and conceptions in Mexico implies the presence of Egyptian priests, and the actual performance of Egyptian rituals guarantees it. As we shall now see, these include all the main types — temple rituals, fertility rituals, and funerary rituals.

On New Kingdom temples the act of censing is frequently to be seen. The manner of using the censor, its actual form, and even its name is remarkably similar in Mesoamerica. In both instances the censor has a long tubular handle with a gripped bowl at one end (Figs.35, 36); the censor is held in one hand and the incense is thrown into it with the other. The Mexican word for incense is *copal.* The same word appears in Ancient Egypt. Dioscorides in

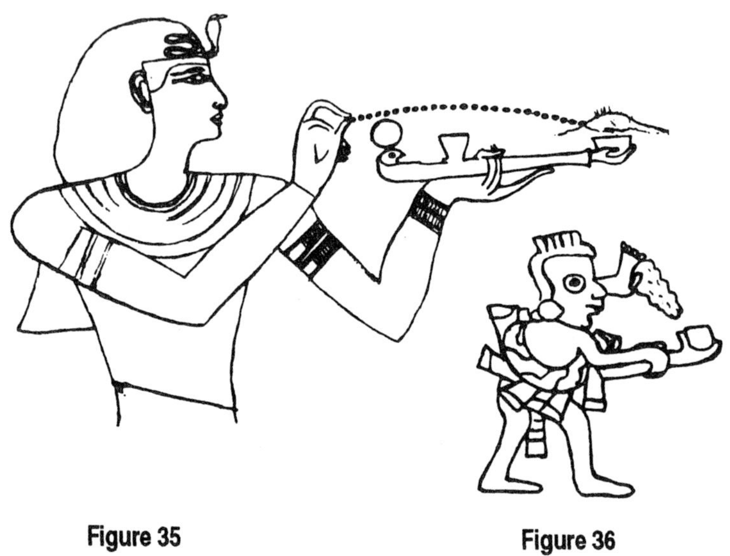

Figure 35 **Figure 36**

the 1st Century A.D. says that Copal was the exudation of a wood like myrrh.

The Maya Epic the *Popol Vuh* says in so many words that the ancestors who first came across the seas from the sunrise "untied the incense they had brought from there."[21] This recalls the pictures on temple walls of incense trees being carried on board Egyptian ships in foreign lands.

Figure 37 Figure 38

Again fertility cults involving the phallus correspond in minute particulars. In both cases erect artificial phalli were either worn or carried by initiates. According to Herodotus they were one cubit long, which is 20.6 inches.[22] An Olmec stone phallus is *exactly* this length, and in a Mexican Codex (Fig.37) the artificial phalli are also about this length. In the latter they are holding their erect phalli just like the Egyptian god Min (Fig.38). Both the Mexican and Egyptian cults involved processions. And these go back to Olmec times at Chalcatzingo (Fig.39).

The initiates striding toward a phallic figure hold oars. This again is exactly comparable with the Pharaoh holding an oar and running toward the phallic god Min (Fig.40).

Another ritual whose significance is not fully understood was striking a ball with a stick. As this picture shows (Fig.42), the balls are being returned

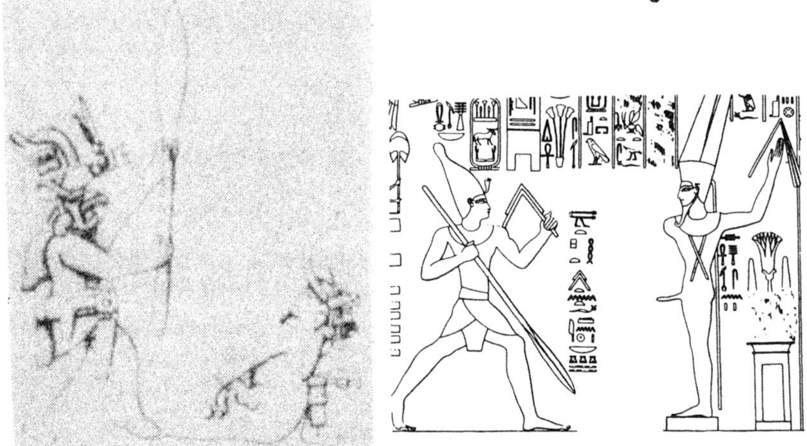

Figure 39

Figure 40

to the Pharaoh by ball-boys to enable him to repeat the act. By this act, the text says, the king was "making a given life."[23] We know that in Mexico too the priests struck stone balls with a stick. This proves that as in Egypt it was a ritual rather than a game. Here is a West Mexican figurine with ball and stick (Fig.41). Notice both wear a twin-feathered head-dress — surely not a coincidence when such a ritual was practised nowhere else in the world.

Egyptian priests also performed funerary ceremonies that were known nowhere else but in Mexico. This libation (Fig.43) was performed over the Pharaoh; its purpose was to restore his fluid in

Figure 41

Figure 42

the afterlife.[24] Streams of water are poured from two vases which cross over the head. This is just what occurs in the Mexican codex (Fig. 44), and again it has to do with the afterlife as they are all Underworld gods. We know that the lords of Chalco had libations poured on the heads of their desiccated mummies to restore to them the water which they had used in

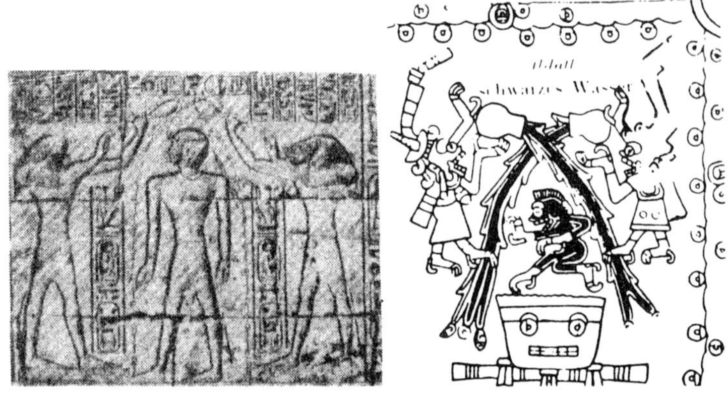

Figure 43

Figure 44

their life.

Chief among faculties that Egyptian priests hoped to restore to the dead was *speech*. There were two ritual acts involved, and both occur in Mexico. In one an implement was applied to the mouth, and the ceremony was called "the opening of the mouth". Here it is pictured in the Egyptian *Book of the Dead* (Fig.45), and in this Olmec painting deep in the cave at Juxtlahuaca (Fig.46). In both cases the priests wear jaguar or leopard skin robes with the tail of the animal hanging between their legs. Both extend a snake-like implement toward the kneeling figure of the deceased. In Egypt the opening of the mouth could also be achieved by touching the mouth of the dead or his statue with the bleeding foreleg of the bull. In the same way we know from the Maya

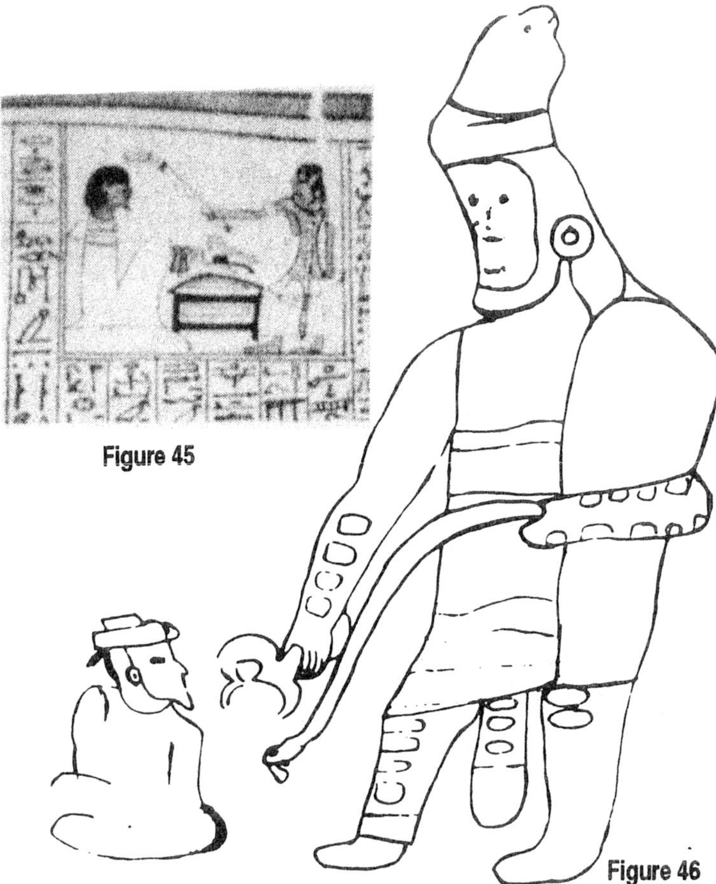

Figure 45

Figure 46

book the *Popol Vuh* that the people who came across the sea from the sunrise could make a statue speak by touching its mouth with the blood of deer and birds. So this is yet another instance where artifacts show the parallels, and texts confirm that the practice was introduced from overseas.

According to the *Popol Vuh* there were not only worshippers among the first men who came across the sea from the sunrise, but sacrificers as well. Could this have included heart sacrifice? Heart sacri-

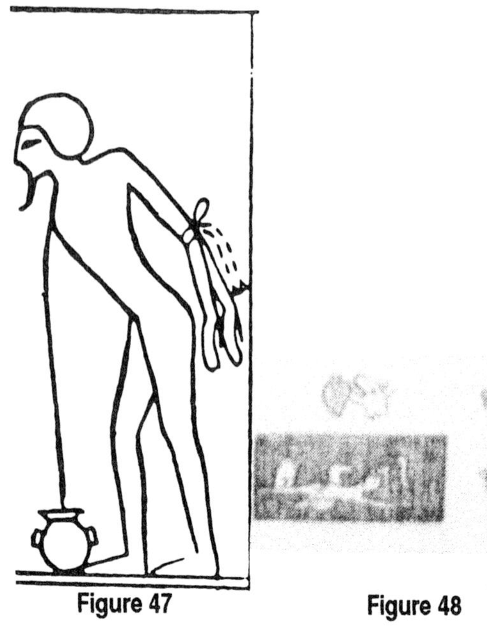

Figure 47 Figure 48

fice was not literally practised in Egypt, though all the elements were there in the texts. In Mexico the heart was plucked out and offered to the sun. In Egypt these hearts which were plucked out (Fig. 47) are those of the enemies of the sun god. In Mexico the heart is devoured by a beast (Fig.48) in the penultimate stage in the Underworld. In Egypt the heart was devoured by the monster Amemit (Fig.49) if its sins outweighed the truth on the scale. In Mexico the goddess Tlazolteotl eats the sins of men when they confessed to her once in their lifetime.[26] It is possible to imagine how out of mythological elements, a real practice could arise.

So much for priests. What is the evidence for scribes? It was usual to send scribes on Egyptian expeditions, and we know of one such instance in the reign of Rameses IV. Sahagun records that the first ancestors who came to Mexico across the seas had 'bookmen' among them.[27] But he says most of them

Figure 49:

went away leaving only four wise men to govern. They had to make a fresh start and contrive a calendar, knowing only that such things existed, for as Sahagun says, the bookmen had gone away taking with them their writings, the books, the paintings, the crafts and the casting of metals. We know that the Olmecs were the first in the Americas to introduce hieroglyphic writing. And their scribes have visible similarities with the Egyptian. In this relief (Fig. 50) the Olmec teacher is shown in the

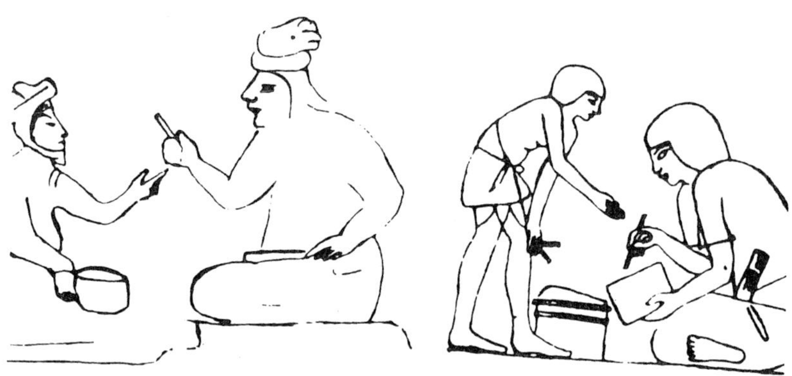

Figures 50, 51

same profile manner as the Egyptian (Fig. 51), and in each case the pupil is pointing to the writing hand of his master. And here again the Olmec counterpart (Fig.53) of the Egyptian scribe (Fig.52) is so similar, that the kilt makes the same oval over the knees, and the rendering of the wig could not be more alike. It is a fair assumption that the scribes would have

Figure 52

Figure 53

taken their patron god Thoth with them (Fig.54), for he was "secretary of Ra in the solar barque."[28] Thoth was represented with a human body and an ibis bill. And this jade statuette (Fig.55) from the Olmec heartland is such a bird-beaked man. He has what could be a stylus over the bill — at least it points straight down to an inscription — almost the earliest example known of the long count inscription which the Mayas later adopted for their dates. The introductory glyph above

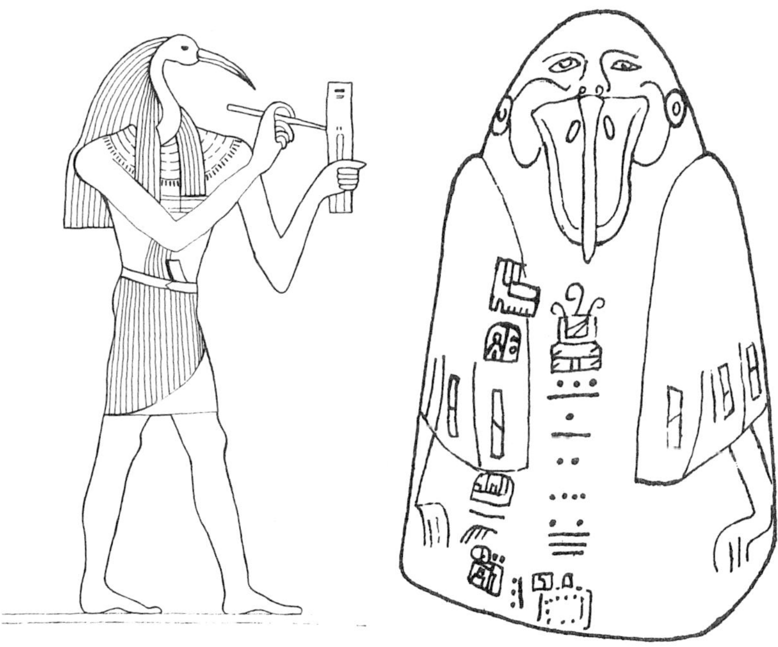

Figures 54, 55

with waves. And another thing — nowhere was the ibis sacred but in Egypt and in Mexico,[29] and its name Ototl is strikingly similar to the Egyptian Thoth.

Later we shall see one Egyptian hieroglyph in use among the Olmecs which had the very same meaning.

There appear to have been Levantines among the Olmec migrants. This dignitary on an Olmec stele (Fig.56) is bearded and has an aquiline nose. His lineage is further suggested by one of the retainers above who raises an index finger — an exclusively Levantine gesture signifying homage.[30] He

Figures 56, 57

fits the description of Torquemada who says that the chief of the people who came from the north via Panuco ('the place where they landed') was fair and had a beard.

But why should he have a fish in his head-dress unless it symbolises the sea? This question is investigated in Appendix I, and it is concluded that it is likely to be the Abtu fish that swims in the bow of the ship of the sun God. This possibility should be entertained in view of the solar voyage. At any rate it is not surprising to find Syrians among the personnel of Egyptian ships. A delegation of Syrians is to be seen in the Tomb of Rameses III (Fig. 57), and if they were Babylonian this might explain the presence of the Babylonian traits in Olmec Mexico which include the stepped temple or ziggurat, cylinder seals, and a sequence of myths to do with the Creation, the Destruction, and the Flood.[31]

Ubiquitous among the Olmecs are Africoid types. Nowhere but in Egypt at the time were Levantines and black Africans intermingled.[32] The colossal Olmec heads clearly represent Africans. This is one of a over dozen so far excavated (Fig. 58). All of them have broad noses and thick, fleshy lips, quite unlike the native Indians. Examination of Olmec skulls by a Polish anthropologist has independently detected a strong "Africoid" element.[33] Proof that they are not just Africans, but blacks from *Egypt* is that nowhere else at the time were African heads

Figures 58, 59

are Ramessid Nubian heads from Tanis (Fig.59), which was the port from whence expeditions were sent on the Mediterranean.[34] The resemblance extends to the incised parallel lines on the leather helmet. The other undoubted stamp of Egypt is that nowhere else at the time were colossal sculptures being carved and transported miles from their quarries. Here they were brought fifty miles, though some of them weighed as much as forty tons. The powerful portraits testify that they are persons in authority. The technique of monumental stone carving did not exist in Mexico before the Olmec advent. I now think that some among the Nubian crew may have been ship's captains; remember that the leader of Hathshepsut's Punt expedition was called 'Nahasi', the Nubian.[34a] We know also that on Rameses III's Punt expedition were ship's captains, inspectors and petty officers.[34b]

To conclude — with the aid of texts and comparative evidence from both sides, I have been able to surmise who were some of the people that took part in the great voyage to the West: they included Egyptian priests, Nubians, and Levantines.

PART III

GODS FROM MORNING TO MIDNIGHT

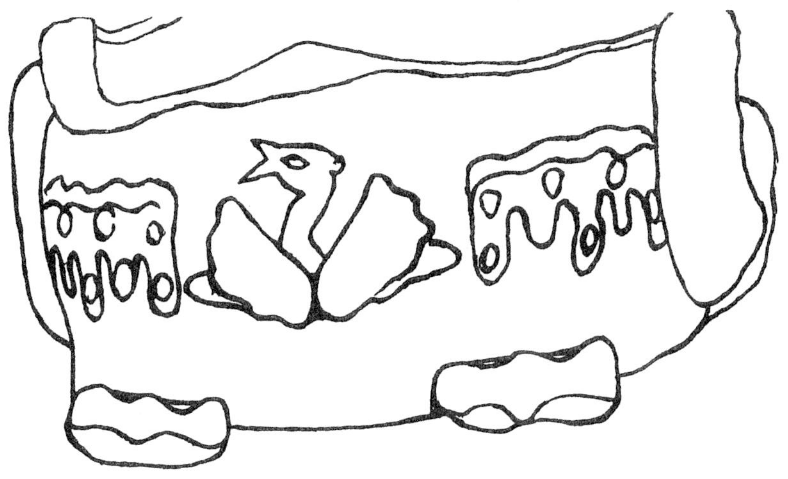

Figure 60

At the beginning of time the waters of chaos engulfed the world. A bird flew up out of the waters and broke the silence with a cackle. This is how Egyptian myth conceives the first sound on earth.[35] This Olmec water basin (Fig.60) depicts a bird rising out of the water — its mouth wide open as though cackling. On either side of it are what look like hills of unbridled water, surely a graphic way of describing the waters of chaos. The basin itself is in the form of a duck; could it not be the Egyptian god, "the Great Cackler"? At any rate, the Mexican picture is as exact a rendition of the Egyptian text as one can imagine. There was a later Mexican festival described by Sahagun in which men jumped into the water and began to cackle like ducks and other birds.[36] As this was during the course of a festival, it compellingly recalls the Egyptian *Book of the Dead* which says "I cackle like the *smen* goose... on the festival of the great being."[37]

Another monumental basin of Olmec date leads us once again back to Egypt and to the beginnings of things. An enormous stone basin was planted in the heart of the stepped pyramid of Totimihuacan near Puebla, one of the earliest such structures in the Americas. The basin is in a small room reached by a sloping corbel-vaulted corridor. What intriguing ceremonies went on here! There are frogs carved along the rim (Fig.61). A basin with frogs carved along the rim occurs nowhere else but in Egypt (Fig.62). In Egypt the frog was a symbol of birth, and if the same meaning were implied by its counterpart, then the room in the pyramid could be a birth room. If so, this would be yet another link with Egypt, since there were birth rooms in Egyptian

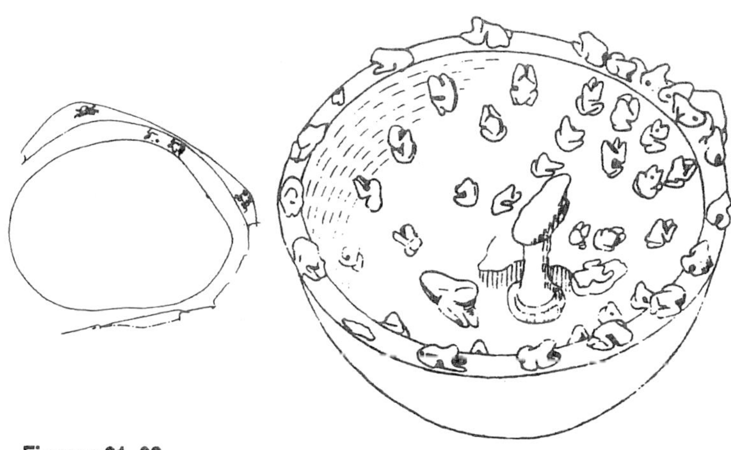

Figures 61, 62

temples, and the *Book of the Dead* speaks of the renewal of youth by being born in the birth room of Osiris.[38]

We shall now pursue the cycle of the sun from its rising and setting, to its death and rebirth. What if I were to show that at every stage there are remarkable and precise parallels, would this not rule out any doubt whatever that the mission had been inspired by this very purpose, and that in fact it had been a solar voyage?

The cycle began in the first flush of dawn at the emergence of the sun. The helpers of the sun in Egypt danced and sang and praised and shouted. So in Mexico dead warriors shouted as the sun emerged. And the Maya Epic tells that the ancestors who had come across the sea from the East performed a dance at sunrise.[39]

The Egyptians pictured the sun as passing through the body of the sky goddess Nut. Her body splits in two at the thighs (Fig.65), and the sun emerges from her vulva (Fig.64), as the text says, and as is seen on the ceiling in the tomb on Rameses VI. Compare this Mexican goddess (Fig. 63) from a codex or picture book. She also is upside down, her legs do the splits,

Figures (left to right): 63. 64,65.

and the young sun emerges. The sequence of identical ideas rules out coincidence.

And further, the sky was thought to be supported in identical fashion. In Egyptian myth it was supported at its corners by four gods who had been created while the world was still deluged.[40] These are the sky supporters on a Ramessid altar (Fig.66). In Maya myth also there are four support gods, the Bacabs, and moreover, they supported the four points of the

Figure 66

world which had been deluged. These Olmec (Fig.67) supporters (in art history they are referred to as Atlantes after Atlas) actually uphold symbols which are none other than the Egyptian hieroglyph for "the sky." This is the goddess Nut (Fig.68) supporting her own sky-sign. In Egypt it had not been treated simply as a myth, but was actually celebrated in an annual festival called "Uplifting of the Sky."

Figures 67, 68

The Egyptians conceived the dawning sun as a child. Texts describe him as "child of the sky who dawns in the bow of his ship, and sails with the king to the horizon in the bark of Ra." He is "Horus the child, the babe with the finger in his mouth."[41] Here he is on the sun's ship in Rameses' Temple (Fig. 69). And this Olmec terracotta baby (Fig.70) is not just any baby. He too must be the solar child since he has a star perforated in his head, a finger in his mouth, and Mexican texts describe the emerging sun at dawn as "the beautiful child."[42] This surely explains why the baby was such a ubiquitous theme among the Olmecs.

Another aspect of Horus in Mexico was as an eagle

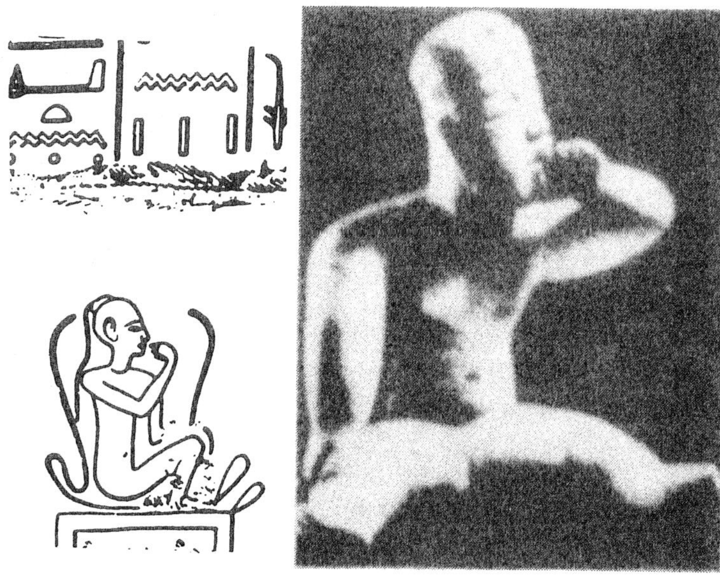

Figures 69, 70

flying toward the West. In this Mexican codex the eagle has reached the crater in which the sun goes down and where the Underworld begins (Fig.71). The picture fits the Egyptian text which describes the Egyptian god Horus as the "great falcon whose flight has reached the ramparts of the horizon."[43] There were Horus falcons in full flight on the masts of Rameses III's ship, and as far as I know, of no other Pharaoh.

Figure 71

One extraordinary conception in Egypt shown in the Tomb of Rameses IX (Fig. 72) is that of goddesses of the West who caught the sun in their arms and took it down into the Underworld. Aztec literature describes women who lived at the falling place of the sun, who caught the sun in their arms, and carried it in their hands, brought it down, and left it where it enters the Underworld.[44] The Mexican description could well be

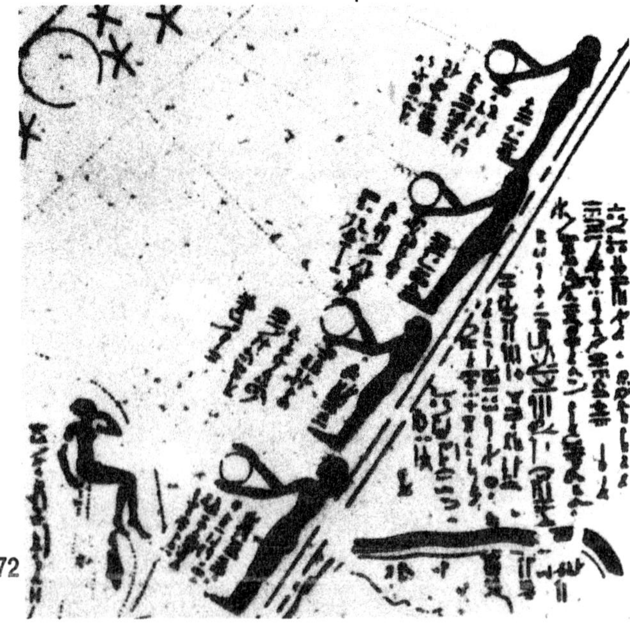

Figure 72

an accurate caption to the Egyptian picture!

Notice the scarab beetle standing on end in this same picture. Another Mexican text asks: "What is the black stone standing on its head as if listening to the land of the dead?" Back comes the answer, "It is the beetle." If we in turn ask: "Where are there known to have been black stone beetles?" The answer is — "In the Temple of Rameses III."[45] Monumental stone beetles were unknown outside Egypt.

The ship of the sun did not have an easy time setting. A serpent attacks it, but the god Seth successfully slays it, as depicted in this Egyptian picture (Fig.73). Time and again Rameses III is

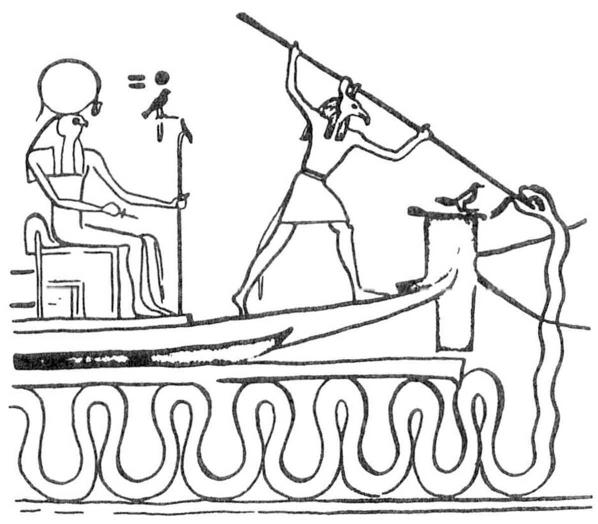

Figure 73:

compared to "Seth slaying the robber serpent on the prow of the evening barque."[46] Here on an early Mexican relief at Izapa (Fig. 74) is a god slaying a serpent which is about to swallow a barque. The curlicue Izapan style should not blind one to what is going on. Stylistic change there may be, but the content is the same in both.

Figure 74:

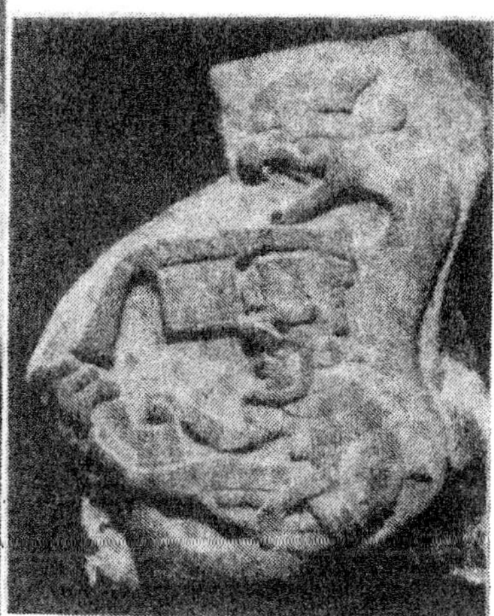

Figures 75, 76

Now an important event occurs from our point of view. As the sun's ship enters the Underworld, it turns upside down. This is clear on the ceiling of the Tomb of Seti I (Fig.75). Here it is the right way up, and then after the sky goddess swallows it, it becomes upside down. This is the Olmec version, (Fig. 76) scarcely recognisable, but quite unmistakable with reed clumps on the prow and an empty cabin, and crosses on the hull symbolic of the Underworld. A great serpent arches over a god or man. He could be the personified mountain Manu which the Egyptian *Book of the Dead* describes as having a gigantic serpent 50 cubits long with flint-like jaws arching over its top.[47] The two things taken together — the over-arching snake and the upside down boat — should be coupled with the knowledge that Rameses III yearned to go to Manu, and sent his ships to 'the inverted waters.'[48]

What transpired when the Egyptian sun god Ra entered the Underworld and came face to face with its chief god, Osiris? We are told that they united[49] and this is shown usually by combining the lower half of one god with the upper half of the other (Fig.77).

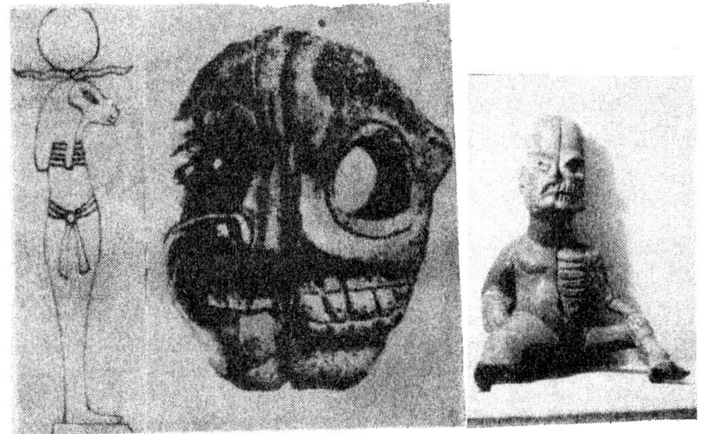

From left to right: Figures 77, 78, 79

The same two gods are physically combined in Mexico, only laterally rather than vertically. In this Mexican version (Fig.78) the skeletal Underworld god is on the right, and the sun god on the left recognisable by his usual attribute, the hanging tongue. And again the two are united into one in this Olmec terracotta (Fig.79). Since one half of the figure has to be solar, this proves that the child in Olmec art must refer to the solar child (cf. above, Figs.69, 70).

Another thing that happens to Osiris is that as the sun's boat comes near him in the Underworld he revives and raises his head[50] or, in other words, he is resurrected (Fig.80). This Olmec sculpture with a powerful Africoid face must again be Osiris (Fig.81); he too lies prone and raises his head in a manner unknown elsewhere in the world's art.

Figure 80:

Figure 81:

Osiris performs an acrobatic feat in papyrus paintings (Fig.82). His body forms a loop, and his feet touch his head. Terracottas performing this feat were placed beside the dead in cemeteries of Olmec date in highland Mexico (Fig.83) This one has Africoid features. In the Egyptian context Osiris signified the circuit of the Underworld,[51] and by this token this figure in the Olmec tomb probably implies that the deceased is travelling through the Underworld circuit protected by its god.

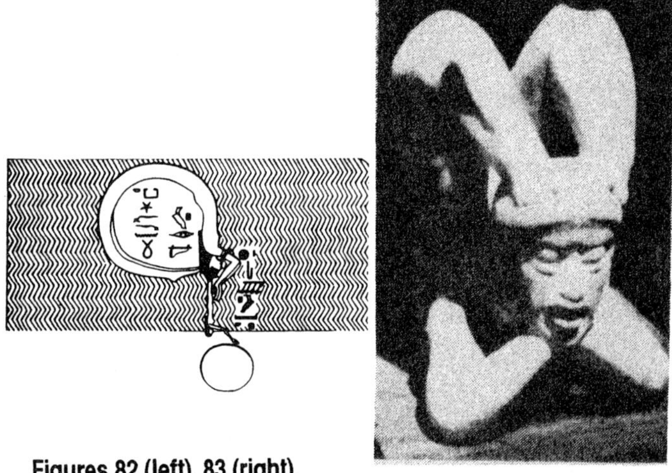

Figures 82 (left), 83 (right).

The next event is dramatically portrayed in this Mexican picture from *Codex Borgia* (Fig. 84). The sun is darkened and dies. He lies spread-eagled — his speech and breath cut off. But in the coils of the fire serpent (Fig.85) there is a rekindling. Then the new sun travels through the serpent with the help of

Figure 84

Figure 85

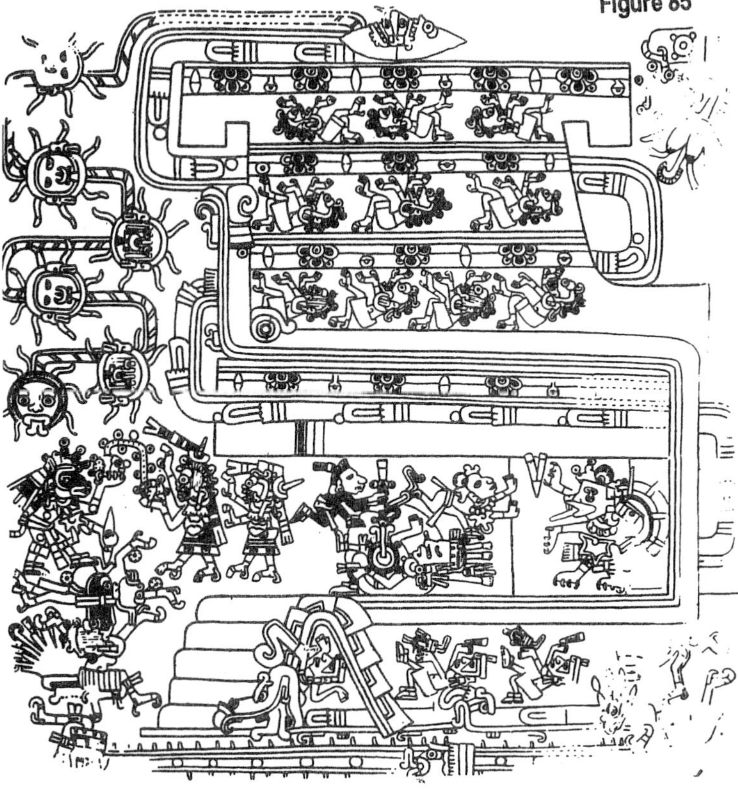

twelve sceptre women (Ciuateteos), and emerges at the top through a stone knife in the serpent's tail. As he rises his first act is to demolish the multiheaded demon of darkness, Tzitzimime "those who fell head-first." This whole sequence of episodes is drawn from Egyptian texts;[52] the sun dies, is refilled with fire during the night, is hauled through the body of the serpent by twelve women called Amkhiu who assist it on the paths of the sky, and Ra's first act is to demolish Apophis (the serpent) so that it plunges into the abyss with face overturned.

The evidence I have just mustered justifies the conclusion that the Egyptians had brought a host of gods with them mainly to do with the sun and the Underworld since these were their two chief objectives. Is this corroborated by native texts? Yes, partly. That respected chronicler Sahagun reports that the first people who came to this country brought with them a god called Coyotlinauatl, and on festival days they dressed the image of this god in a coyote skin.[53] Just as these people worshipped the prairie wolf, so the Egyptians (and no other people) worshipped its equivalent, the jackal, and they wore its mask, as this terracotta (Fig.86) conclusively proves. .

One final question — why, if the Egyptians had brought their gods with them, should they now have assumed different names? Once again the answer lies in the *Popol Vuh*. It says that the first people who

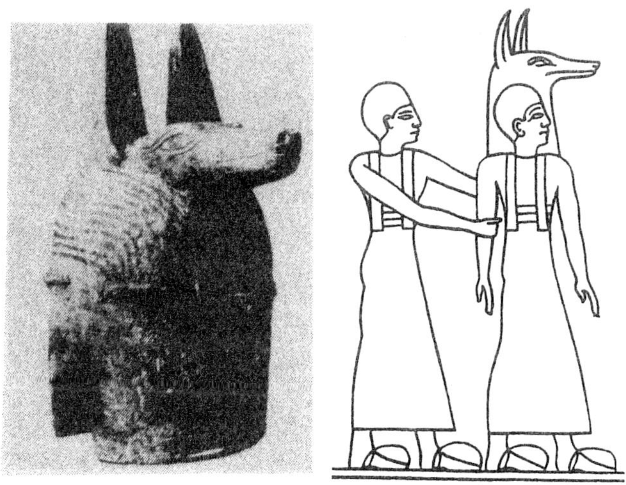

Figure 86

came to their land across the sea from the sunrise brought their scriptures with them, and the name of their gods were changed after they had come.[54]

PART IV

PILGRIMS TO THE LAND OF BLISS

Unlike ancient Babylonians, the Egyptians had an optimistic belief in the Afterlife: a land of promised bliss awaited them, though the way that led there was full of hazards. To negotiate past these hazards, one had to have a guide to the infernal regions. One of these was called "The Book of Traversing Eternity." Small sheets or strips of papyrus of this book were placed in the coffin with the deceased.

This highly unusual practice was transmitted to Mexico; priests delivered bunches of paper to the dead, telling them that this would enable them to survive the encounters in the Underworld.[55]

The entrance to the Egyptian Underworld was the place where the sun went down — that was in the mountain Manu, in the Far West. Reaching this place, the falcon-headed god, Horus perches on the mountain, and is shown in this picture (Fig.87) being worshipped by the Western goddess. The mountain is conceived as a symmetrical undulating mound. The first mound erected by the Olmecs at La Venta, near the south east shores of the Gulf of Mexico, was just

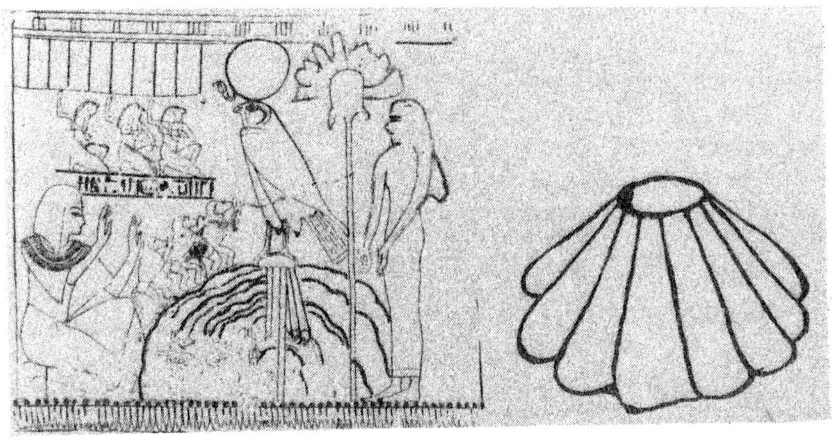

Figure 87, 88

such a symmetrical, undulating mound (Fig.88).

The jaguar mosaic pavements buried inside prove that it was conceived as a solar mound, since the jaguar Tepeyollotl was the god of the sun at night.

This proves that the La Venta mound had the same form and the same meaning as in Egypt. It has been suggested by its excavators that it was intended to be a surrogate or substitute for a mountain.[56] This is perfectly in accord with my view that it was a substitute for Manu and its equivalent St. Martin, within whose crater the monumental sculpture had been discovered (see above Fig.5). At La Venta the mound would have served as a new focal point for the ceremonial centre.

The scheme of the Underworld as preserved by the priests of Chalco in Mexico concurs to an extraordinary degree with that of Egypt.[57] Here are the comparisons in detail:

⁎ The first stage in Mexico is the passage of the dead between two mountains that confront each other. The first stage in Egypt is a mountain with two peaks that lies at the horizon (cf. Figs.6 and 48).

⁎ The second stage in Mexico was guarded by a large snake. The second division in Egypt was guarded by the serpent in the form of Seti.

⁎ The third stage in Mexico was held by an alligator. A crocodile guarded the seventh division in Egypt.

⁎ The fourth stage in the Mexican Underworld was a tract of desert called "eight deserts." The fourth division in Egypt was also a desert region. It was called Seker, and was supported by a sphinx. Here is an Olmec sphinx (clearly it is a man-headed lion), and what's more it is serving as a support (Fig.89).

Figure 89

⁎ In the fifth division in Egypt was the god Aken who counted out the twelve hours of the night (Fig.90). He did this by letting out and swallowing a double rope. This Olmec creature (Fig.91) is literally letting out a double rope from his mouth, and is even more faithful to the Egyptian text than the Egyptian picture. It must mean that this idea was transmitted orally.

⁎ The sixth stage in Mexico was called "winds like obsidian blades." The sixth division in Egypt was the city gate with sharp knives. What is an obsidian blade but a sharp knife!

Above: Figure 90, below: Figure 91

⁕ The eighth division in Egypt was an aquatic zone (Fig.92) in which its inhabitants swam though submerged, and moved toward the primeval flood. Such a realm is pictured in a Mexican wall painting (Fig. 93) from Teotihuacan (before the 7th Century AD).

The deceased are swimming in and around a watery mountain which could well be descriptive of the primeval flood. In this paradise called Tlalocan, the inmates can't drown — and to prove it one figure is actually rescuing another.

So we have seen in almost every stage of the Underworld precise parallels and identical sequences.

Above : Figure 92, below: Figure 93

There can be no doubt that the priests of Chalco had preserved their ancestral system almost intact.

Quite apart from the *way* that lay through the Underworld being the same on both sides, the description of the final bliss was again the same — not once, twice, but at least six times. Just as there was no attempt to unify the different conceptions, or reduce the possibilities in Egypt, so this too was the case in Mexico, and all the different conceptions coexisted. The three that we have met before are "the land of corn," "the metamorphosis into stars," and "the swimmers who do not drown."[58] Here are three more:

⁕ First is the paradisal tree. Other cultures may have a special tree in paradise, but here there are detailed correspondences, and the context and the conception are the same in both. On the lid of the

Figures 94, 95

sarcophagus found within the pyramid of Palenque, the deceased Maya ruler is shown resting under the shade of a tree (Fig.94). So on the lid of an Egyptian sacophagus is a text referring to the Ished tree,[59] and New Kingdom Pharaohs, including Rameses III, are shown on temple walls (Fig. 95) seated under the shade of the Ished tree. The name itself — Ished, approximates Yakshe. Landa describes the dead Mayas as resting under the cool shade of the Yakshe tree forever.[60] Egyptian texts describe the dead lying under the sycamore tree. [61]

⁕ Another conviction of the ancient Egyptians was that the deceased would re-emerge from his/her tomb in a new bodily form and visit the earth. This form would be as a Ba, a harpy or human-headed bird. Here the Ba is emerging from a hole in the tomb, and is about to fly up to the surface (Fig. 96). And again in this Mexican relief from Izapa a human-headed bird is flying up out of a cavern.

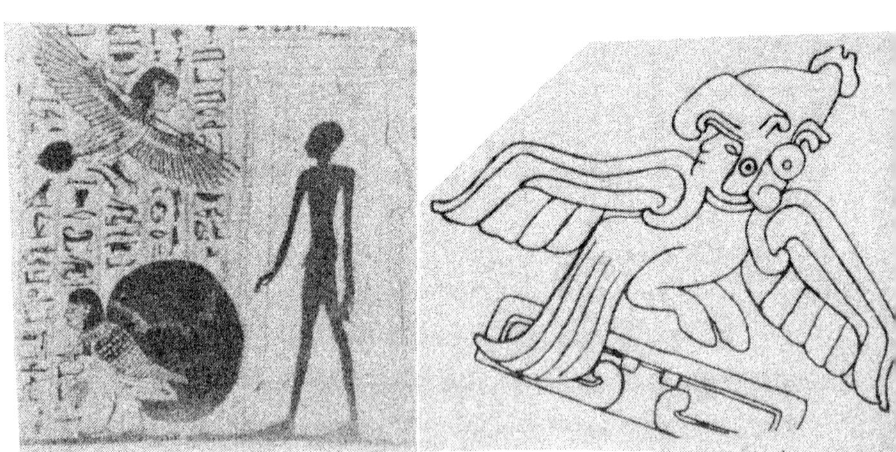

From left: Figures 96, 97

✱ And lastly the Egyptian belief that the deceased would become "a glorious one" was transmitted to Mexico. Indeed, the *Popol Vuh* says in so many words that when the ancestor who had come across the sea from the sunrise died, he left behind his sign, his essence called "the shrouded glory."[62] This Olmec lord, seated in a niche (Fig.98), would have achieved this state. He corresponds to the description of 'those who have reached the West and become horizon-dwellers.'[63] The Egyptian text says they are 'lords of the caverns seated in their holes, which is a good description of this figure.

Figure 98

The text says that they hold ropes in their hand; so does this figure. The *Book of the Dead* says they have four flaming torches, and calls them "the shining ones."[64] This is surely a marvellously evocative description of this Olmec person who sits flanked by four torches and shines out against the dark background of the Underworld cavern.

CONCLUSION

I have reviewed some of the parallels between Ancient Egypt and Mexico. There are a great many more; and they are *exclusive* to the two lands. They are supported by every kind of evidence - archaeological, historical, mythological, ritual, literary and artistic. It is now crystal clear who was instrumental, and how the whole thing was accomplished, and what it achieved.

All the evidence points to just *one person* who engineered the whole thing, and it was at the juncture of a sequence of events. This person was Rameses 111; the event was his defeat of the Sea Peoples. He accomplished this by building a great fleet in the Mediterrarean; it consisted of warships, galleys and coasters. After the war was over, he sent the fleet on an expedition and was the *only* Pharaoh to have claimed this. It was precisely at the time that his pronouncement was made that Olmec civilization sprang up in Mexico.

Great civilizations though they were in their own right, there was a time once when Egypt and Mexico were close cousins. Together they took part in an amazing adventure which changed the course of history. This new civilization that emerged in turn affected its neighbour to the north, and now we shall attempt to discover precisely in what manner.

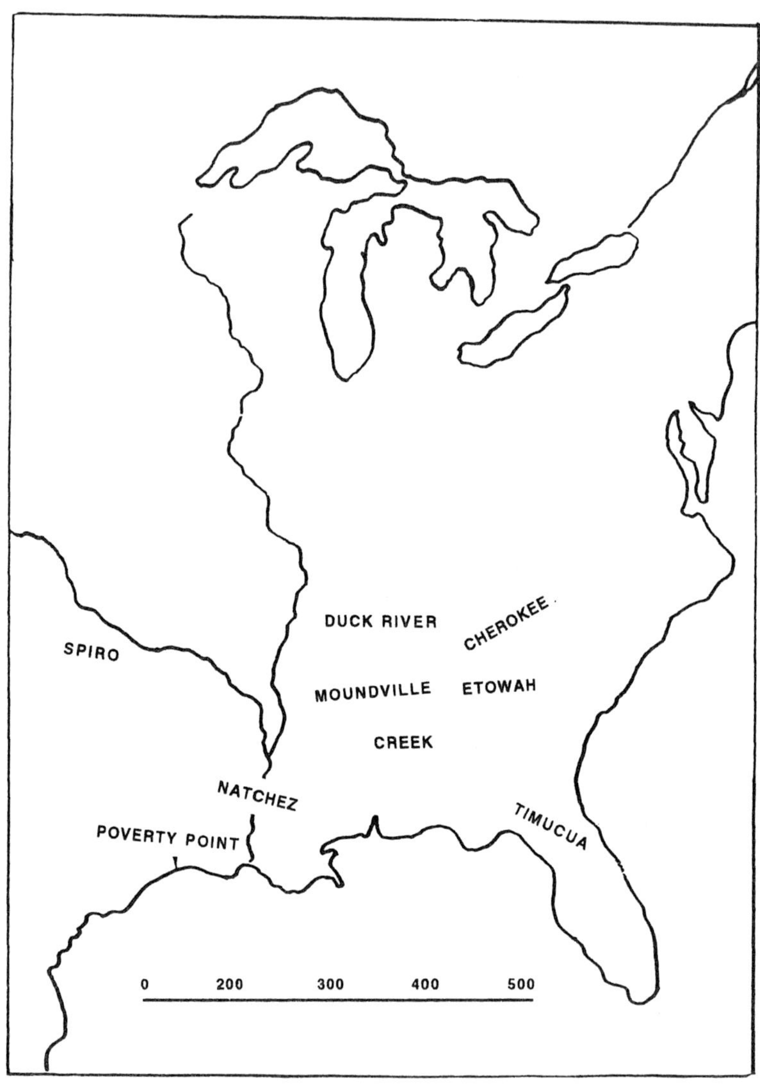
DUCK RIVER
CHEROKEE
SPIRO
MOUNDVILLE
ETOWAH
CREEK
NATCHEZ
POVERTY POINT
TIMUCUA
0
200
300
400
500

CHAPTER 2

ANCIENT EGYPTIAN & MEXICAN PRESENCE IN SOUTH EAST UNITED STATES

Pioneering work

As early as 1884 William Holmes pointed out that repoussé designs on copper plates found in Illinois and northern Georgia were "suggestive of Mexican and Central American designs."[1] He later pointed to the presence of copper bells found occasionally in southern states as having reached Florida from Mexico.[2]

In 1932 Zelia Nuttal showed some resemblances between copper plates from Etowah and Mexican iconography, including figures wearing bird masks,[3] and attributed this to migration from Mexico resulting from "volcanic disturbances, droughts, grasshopper plagues followed by famine."

In 1953 Krieger referred to parallels between Mexican Codex figures and some shell gorgets from Spiro, eastern Oklahoma, and went on to postulate migrations between Mesoamerica and the eastern United States on several different time levels, beginning possibly from the Christian era and continuing until nearly the time of the conquest, or later.[4]

In 1966 Gordon Willey admitted Mesoamerican affiliation in the assemblage, including forked or "weeping" eye, a cross with a sunburst circle, god-animal representations, masked men impersonating animals, serpents, eagles and cats.[5] The question of whether mound-building was introduced from Mexico bas been debated. In 1965 James Griffin wrote that there was nothing in Mesoamerica resembling the large earth conical mound and multiple octagon at Poverty Point in north east Louisiana in the period 800 - 600 B.C., and argued that in Mesoamerica there were only truncated pyramids as substructures, and functionally also they were different. He however agrees that clay figurines of the same date, 800 - 600 B.C., may have come from

Mexico,[6] also ear spools.[7] He further maintains that Hopewell clay figurines (from Ohio, Missouri and north east Oklahoma) have the bent knee stance similar to La Venta Olmec figures. The date, 100 - 300 A.D. cited is too late for La Venta, or even c.200 B.C. - 400 A.D. cited by Willey for Hopewell.[8] Hopewell has panpipes, and these are found in this same time-level (100 B.C. - 300 A.D.) on the Gulf Coast of Mexico. Finger rings of copper were introduced in the earlier Adena phase.[9] In 1978 James Marshall attempted to prove that the unit of measure (about 187 feet) at Teotihuacan is the same as that employed for Hopewell earthworks, and concludes that "small groups of American Indian geometers must have made the trip from Mexico to Ohio as early as 400 B.C."[10]

Agricultural origins indicated the same kind of pattern, and the same range of dates. Mesoamerica transfers maize, beans, squash and gourds to North America in the 1st millennium B.C. Previous to this, Woodland Indians were cultivating a number of indigenous weedy plants notably sunflower, marsh elder, etc., which have been recovered from refuse pits in contexts which suggest that stocks were stored for spring planting.[11] In the estimation of James Griffin, maize was probably introduced c.100 B.C., and gourd and squash somewhat later.[12] Also transmitted from late Formative Mexico is the long bifacial and bipointed ceremonial knife which priest figures carry in Etowah art.[13]

Later inputs from the Mexican area to the eastern United States included negative painting in the late Hopewell period[14] and engraved decoration on pottery (700 -900 A.D.).[15] The practice of pipe-smoking appears to have gone the other way — from the south-east area of the United States to Mexico between 900 and 1400 A.D., according to Porter[16].

So far, following the existing literature, we have seen significant transfers of traits over a wide span of time from Mexico to the United States. Now I shall examine some of the transmitted traits more carefully, and trace their antecedents.[17] Before I try to answer the question of how and why the trait transfers took place within the continent, it is necessary to subject specific traits to iconographic analysis, and see where they lead us.

The winged serpent

Incised on a pot from Moundville, Alabama, is a winged

Figure 99

horned serpent (Fig. 99).[18] One thinks of the feathered serpent in the god Quetzalcoatl of Mexico, but it would be even more relevant to look for a prototype in a *winged* rather than a *feathered* serpent. We find such a serpent in relief in Olmec Mexico at Chalcatzingo (Fig.100). The serpent is devouring a human, half of

Figure 100

whom it has swallowed. It is admitted that what looks like a gill is likely to be a wing, and "if so a feathered serpent is implied".[19]

Seeking still further back in time for the origins of the serpent with wings, we are is led back to Ancient Egypt. On the sarcophagus of Seti I in the Soane Museum (13th century B.C.), two-winged serpents serve as warders,[20] and there are also four-winged serpents.[21] The former type appear in a British Museum Papyrus of c.1100 B.C., where the deceased is seen offering his heart to it (Fig. 101).[22] Earlier still in the Tomb of Rameses III (c. 1136 B.C.), a wall painting shows the Underworld God,

Figure 101

Sokar, standing on the back of a serpent with two wings which the god holds. The epithet of Sokar is 'great god with his two wings opened.'[23] The later development of the theme is of little interest for our purpose, though we should note in passing the comments in Herodotus (II, 74 - 7) about winged serpents being devoured by the ibis. The Americanist Spinden admitted that the closest parallel in the ideal development of the serpent in Maya art was the Egyptian, but opposes any connection with the winged serpent in the Mound Culture.[24] We shall see on the contrary that if Mesoamerica is regarded as a way-station, then there is nothing implausible in there being a lineal connection.

Eagle mask

The eagle mask appears on an embossed copper plate from the Etowah group of mounds (Temple Mound C, Fig.102). Etowah is five miles south of Cartersville in Georgia. Although the Etowah Valley was first occupied c.5000 B.C., most burials in the mortuary complex date from 950 - 1450 A.D. Three hundred and fifty burials with elaborate grave goods were found from the S.W. temple platform.[25] It is admitted that some of the copper plates with stamped figures resemble Mexican designs.[26] The Etowah masked figure has been described as a dancer

Figure 102

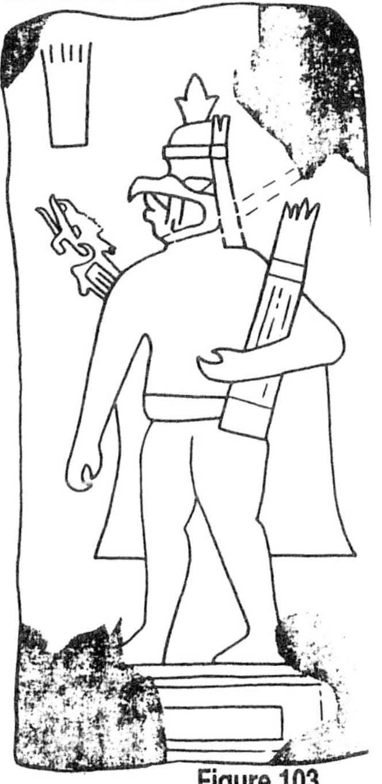

Figure 103

holding in one hand a cross-inscribed baton, and a trophy head in the other.[27] Much further west at the Spiro Mound in Oklahoma, there was found in burial another anthropomorphised hawk engraved on a copper plate; its face was human except for a beak and crest feathers.[28] This beak and crest feather type of eagle mask can be traced back to Olmec Mexico where a cloaked man incised on a stele from San Miguel Amuco[29] bears a quiver-like object while an ophidian head emerges from his other shoulder (Fig. 103), perhaps as an expression of power.

The use of animal masks in cult ceremonies does not exist in the Americas prior to the Olmecs as far as is known, and once again its original home is likely to be in Egypt. In the Osirian Khoiak Festival, priests imper-

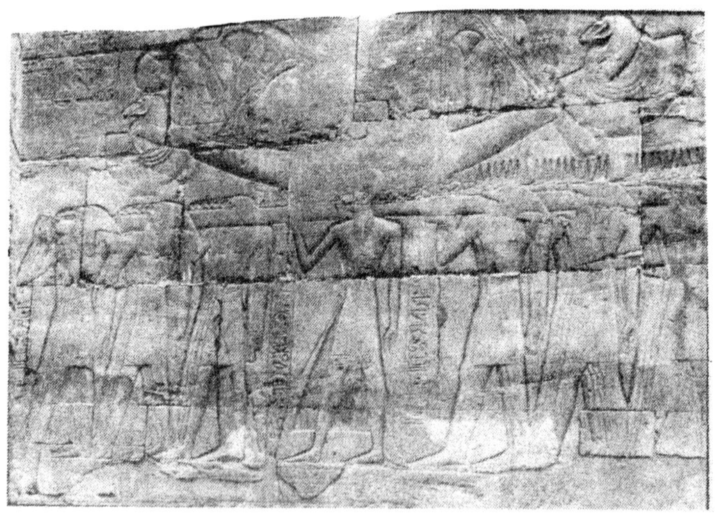

Figure 104

sonated gods by wearing bird or animal masks such as the eagle,ibis, or jackal (Fig. 104).[30] A procession of priests at the Funerary Temple at Madinat Habu of Rameses III shows them wearing lion and eagle masks over their heads (Fig. 105).[31]

Figure 105

Pointed 'pouch'

This feature appears on a number of occasions worn by

persons represented in south-east American Indian art. A Mississipian shell gorget shows a warrior with war club and a trophy head wearing what is described[32] as a pointed pouch which hangs from his waist between his legs (Fig. 106). An embossed copper from Etowah mound has a figure wearing very similar paraphernalia

Figure 106

(Fig. 107), but on this occasion he is thought to be 'a dancer.'[33] A feature of essentially the same form is worn in the same position on the body in Egypt of the time of Rameses III. On one occasion (Fig. 108) it is hung from the waist by a single stick fighter in a sporting contest.[34] On another it is worn by soldiers (Fig.109)

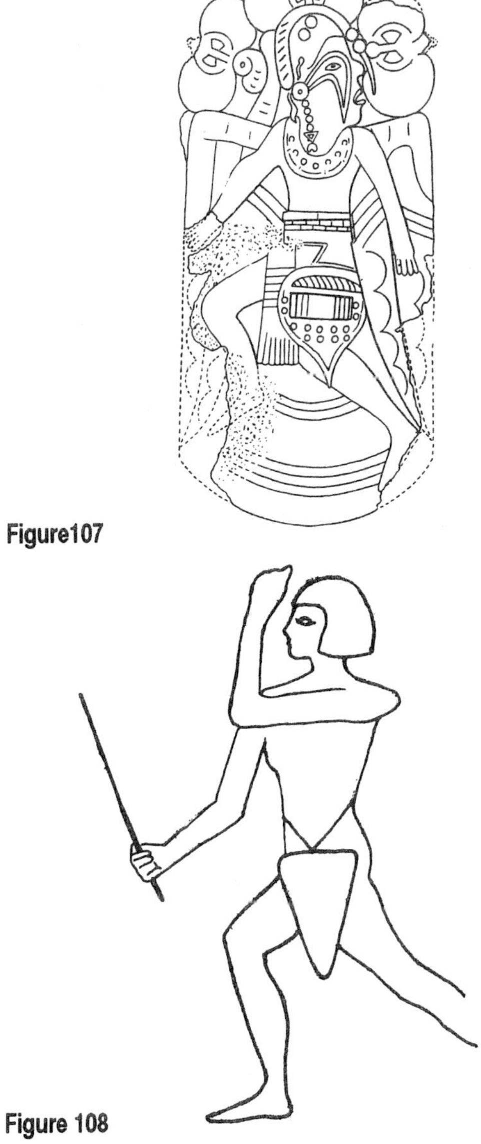

Figure107

Figure 108

helping Rameses III to hunt lions at Madinat Habu.[35] It is clear in this instance that since the shield is held high to cover the head and upper body, the purpose of the pointed device is to serve as a thigh protector, and this must be so also in the former case. If the feature were not found in Mesoamerica, it would be difficult to believe that there is any relation between the 'pouch' of the south-east United States, and the thigh protector of Ramessid Egypt.

However, once again we have an intermediary in Mesoamerica. It is a triangular thigh protector represented on a Guatemalan ballcourt marker. It dates from the late classic 650 - 800 A.D., and is considered to have been of hide or thick cloth.[36] The former is more likely since Father Duran observed that ballplayers in the Aztec period covered their thighs with a protector made of deer skin.[37] I would like to point to another interesting parallel, though I am at present unable to account for it, probably because of the accident of survival of the intermediaries. In Rameses III's funerary temple, the sport of wrestling and single stick fighting are represented below the balcony where the King witnessed it; the balcony is on one side of the court. When De Soto was received by the chief Tascaluca at Athahachi (Mobilian), he says that it was "in a kind of balcony on a mound at one side of a square."[38] One should also remember that the Maya ruler watched the ball game at

Figure 109

Chichen Itza from a balcony which overlooked one side of the ball court.[39]

Figure 110

Figure 111

Cross-in-disk

This symbol is frequently found in south eastern United States art, but neither its meaning nor its origins can be definitely ascertained. Nevertheless, priority of use, points to a possible direction of current.

In at least two instances — in a circular gorget of shell from Charlestown, Missouri[40] (Fig. 110) and in a Mississippian shell gorget with spider design,[41] they were intended to be worn, which is clear from the paired holes, for suspension (Fig. 111). This 'Kan-cross cartouche' is ubiquitous on Maya vases.[42] But it is necessary to reach back much further in time to the Olmec period in Mexico where the symbol appears on the circular eye of an eagle incised on an obsidian core from La Venta[43] (Fig. 112).

Figure 112

Another type of cross, the multiplication (or St Andrews) cross, appears on the eyes of Olmec monuments from Laguna de los Cerros and San Lorenzo. Its recurrence on the head of a person on an Olmec axe from Tapijluapa (Fig. 113)[44] is the most suggestive. There are flames above similar to the flame eyebrow of Olmec iconography.[45] The curved feature between the flame and the disk is extremely reminiscent of the eyebrows of the Horus eye, as for instance in a representation on a papyrus in the *The Book of the Dead* (Fig.114). But

Figure 113

the type of cross-in-disk is related to the hieroglyphic symbol for 'city', which appears over the head of Rameses III in a context referring to the city in the Underworld (Fig. 115).

Figure 114

Figure 115

Stone sculpture

Carved human figures in stone pose something of a problem. There is one type that squats with legs crossed, and at the Etowah site both the male and female are seated in this manner. The female leans forward, probably because of the load she is bearing, which is suggested to be a schematic or symbolic infant on a cradle board.[46] There is a monumental sculpture from Olmec Mexico now in the Jalapa Museum which is seated in the same posture and leans forward, but his arms stretch down to the ground as though he is performing some task, so it could be said that while there is some similarity of form, there is difference in function. In any case, the mode of sitting is common enough, and in this respect no one would claim a direct connection.

There is, however, a different mode of sitting which is comparatively unique in ancient human representations. This is one in which the left knee is bent and the bent leg supports the weight of the body, while the right leg is folded up and helps balance the body. There are scattered examples of this posture in Eastern United States including one from Wilson County in Tennessee of the Mississippi period,[47] another from Temple Mound, Tennessee, suggested to have been a hero figure placed in the mound as an offering [48] (Fig. 116), and yet another from the Eastern States in the Duck River and Gray Cul-

Figure 116 **Figure 117**

ture in which context it is suggested to have been 'the grandfather' of the Muskhogean communities — a special deity connected with the sacred fire and the sun.[49] This mode of sitting is almost exclusive to the art of Ancient Egypt and originates there. Rameses III is shown sitting in this manner not only in his Funerary Temple boating in paradise (see above Fig. 115), but also in his Tomb on a ship heading to the West (Fig. 117). It then appears in an Olmec statue found in a volcanic crater near the Gulf of Mexico, which shares several iconographic features with the same figure of Rameses III[50] (see above p.10).

The feline goddess

Of all the sculptures of PreColumbian south-east United States the little anthropomorphic cougar from Key Marco, Florida,[51] must be the most surprising (Fig. 118). This six inch statuette carved in wood could have been conveniently carried about on the person as protection, since it is evidently a deity. There is nothing quite like it in Mexico where, for example, among the Huastec of the

Figure 118 Figure 119 Figure 120

Gulf Coast, there are stone sculptures seated in similar kneeling poses,but they are all naturalistic figures and not recognizable as gods.[52]

The figure of the feline from Florida recalls the lion-headed goddess Sakhmet from Egypt. The theriomorphic fusion of feline head and human body is typical and characteristic of Egypt, but scarcely anywhere else. Her cult became popular in the 18th Dynasty. Amen-hotep II (c. 1447 - 1421 B.C.) says he set forth in his chariot, and prevailed like Sakhmet over his enemies.[53] Amen-hotep III made as many as 600 stone statues of Sakhmet, many of which survive. "Sakhmet who strikes the Nubians," is inscribed on her black granite statues at the British Museum (Fig. 119). She is the scorching heat of the sun's rays,[54] and in the *Harris Papyrus* of Rameses III she is shown with a solar disk encircled by a uraeus serpent over her head (Fig. 120). A text of Rameses III says that 'the great heat of Sakhmet mingled with their heart, so that their bones burned up in the midst of their bodies.'[55] We will return to this attribute of hers shortly.

If we could present evidence that the feline figure of Florida has not only the same *form* but the same *function* as her counterpart, the identification would be all but complete. Frank Cushing wrote in 1897 that "near the statuette was a large stool, a decayed mask, portions of a short wooden stave, and of symbolic ear-buttons, a sheaf of two dozen throwing arrows, and other remains of warrior-and-hunter-paraphernalia and accoutrements. This affords convincing evidence that the statuette was a deity or god of war or the hunt.'[56]

Moreover, animal-headed humans continued to be represented till late by the Creek Indians, and included wolf, hare, snake, tiger, cat and crocodile. Bartram William wrote in 1789 that they were survivals of something that was of 'greater use and consequence among their ancestors.' He says that the paintings were on clay-plastered walls of the houses especially around the Public Square. In his considered opinion they were 'hieroglyphics or mystical writings, for the same use and purpose as those mentioned by historians to be found on the obelisks, pyramids, and other monuments of the ancient Egyptians, and much after the same style and taste.'[57]

The invasions

In view of the presence of the Egyptian war goddess in Florida, it is legitimate to ask whether there are any other traces of invasion or warfare from the expanding Egypto-Olmec Empire in the Gulf of Mexico. Though I have identified a host of Egyptian deities in the Olmec context (so far numbering 22),[58] the war goddess has been absent, but this could merely be a case of an accident of discovery, for these are early days yet.

I believe that a memory of ancient invasions by sea has been preserved in Cherokee literature in *The Vision of Eloh* which was edited and translated for the first time as recently as 1981.[59] Here follows a summary account:

⁕ When we (the Cherokees) lived beyond the great waters back in the old country, the country was subject to great floods. First they built a great mound, but then they decided to emigrate — they crossed on paths which later become submerged into the deep sea.

They settled and prospered until 'a strange race of men crossed the great waters' and landed warriors who attacked the Cherokees. The Cherokees, destroyed them with their clubs — and sent some of the prisoners back across the water in their canoes as a warning.

⁕ In a few more years another fleet of warriors came across the broad waters armed with bows and arrows, and landed on the shores. Again the Cherokees defeated them, and this time sent the prisoners back in their boats having set fire to their feet with balls of resin.

⁕ At the seven-day dance one of the wise men came out of the temple in the form of an eagle. He predicted that the warriors would not come for another seven years. When they did come again, the Cherokees were ready though many tribes lived far from where the battles took place. They had prepared poison in gourds which made the enemy faint, and thus they defeated the dark invaders.

And from that time till the white man came, they lived in peace.

Before proposing some important conclusions arising from this account, I must repeat a warning expressed by an Americanist in a general context. He says that: 'It is extremely difficult to deduce historical facts from broken accounts. The best for which we may hope at this point in knowledge is to establish a hypothesis which is compatible with the archaeology on the one hand, and with ethnological evidence on the other. Ultimate solutions must await considerable further study.'[60]

This is what I have attempted to do. I have gathered together the archaeological evidence which shows repeated contacts between south east United States, Mexico, and the homeland across the seas, and I have cited a native account which speaks of repeated naval invasions and how they were all repulsed. Oral history has a tendency to telescope events,[61] and perhaps they did not take place in a short span of time as suggested, but over the centuries.

Is it conceivable that there is a reminiscence in the Eloh account of Olmec invasions (remember the reference to 'dark invaders')? Was the strange treatment meted out to them, of setting fire to their feet, and sending them back as warning, deliberately reversing the power of the goddess Sakhmet who is described as 'scorching with flames the feet of enemy soldiers?'[61a] A silver object

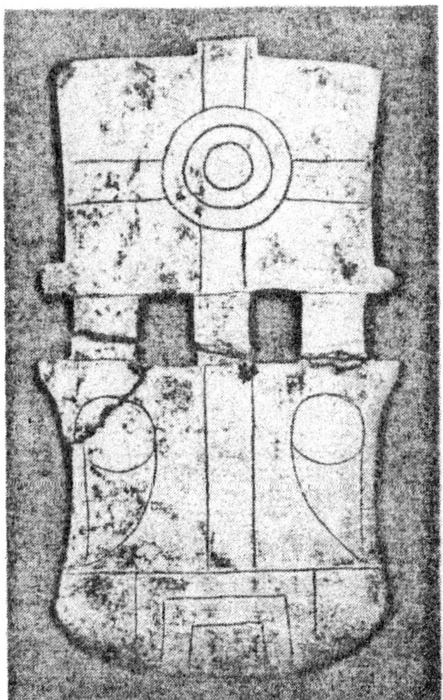

Figure 121

excavated near Lake Okeechobee in Central Florida recalls the Olmec style; it may be compared for instance with monument 15 from La Venta[63] (Fig.121). But the mystery is, who was mining silver at the time? The C-14 date of 1140 B.C. for shell-edge stamping at Bayou La Batre is accepted by two authorities as authentic, but (for no evident reason) not by a third.[64]

The strongest early impact in the south-east is at the Poverty Point site in Louisiana, which is over 200 miles up the Mississippi from the Gulf of Mexico. Radio carbon dates range from c.1200 B.C.. to 400 B.C. According to James Ford, the site has celts of soft green stone related to those of Mesoamerica; also core and blade industry, pottery of female figurines, sandstone saws, and use of solid drills for perforating hard stone.[65] Clarence Webb likewise admits that 'Poverty Point reflects incremental movement of Olmec-derived traits into the lower Mississippi Valley.'[65a] In its form Poverty Point is a wonderfully unique town. It is semi-circular with a diameter of 1.2 kilometres. There were six concentric ridges which were originally interrupted at eight equidistant points. On the West side of the town was a large earth mound 23 metres high; archaeologists maintain that it was in the form of a bird effigy (heading West)[66] (Fig. 122). I endorse this, and elaborate it further in Appendix I. Here I shall only say that the westward flying bird is symbolic, and so also it seems is the circular town with ramparts. My conjecture is that the bird is the Horus falcon whose 'flight has reached the horizon,' as the Egyptian text says,[67] and the circular town is the *sn-wr*, the Great Circle or Okeanis, and Rameses III, who sent his expedition 'to the ends of the earth', says that 'no one escapes him to the ends of the Great Circle.'[68] Since the beginning date of Poverty Point is evidently in the reign of Rameses III, my hypothesis has the merit of contemporaneity. It was, I maintain, a realisation in three dimensions of concepts originating in Egypt and culminating in south-east United States immediately afterward.

The two basic plan forms at Poverty Point — the semi-circle and the oval appear to have been deliberate (and so possibly symbolic). This is suggested by the fact that they were repeated elsewhere within the culture of this

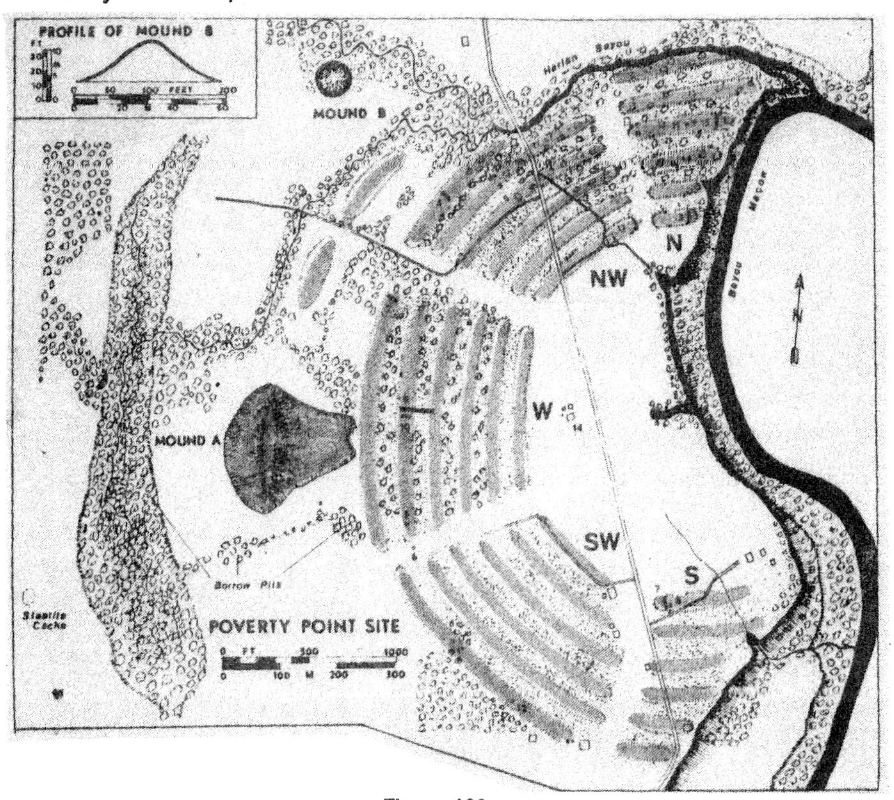

Figure 122

period — for example, a semi-circle of 900 feet diameter in Carroll County, Mississippi, and an oval mound of 22 feet at greatest diameter at Jaketown.[69]

A long-distant memory of mound-building and of immigrants survives in Creek legend. It tells of a time in the dim past of two mounds of earth in the forks of Red River, west of Mississippi where lived three Creek communities who were at a loss for fire. Then there came four men from the corners of the world who made them fire, and the visitors also pointed out to them a number of (named) plants[70]. According to Creek tradition the oldest of their ethnic groups came from the Creek sea shore.[71] These immigration traditions therefore admit that they achieved a higher state of economy and culture as a result of contact with foreign U .S. visitations.

In the Creek confederacy the Natchez language was spoken. It is among these Natchez that the eagle continued to be a dominant symbol. Du Pratz observed that the temple of the Natchez in Louisiana had a ridge pole on its roof on which there were three great birds carved on flat pieces of wood. They were twice as large as a goose, and had no feet. These birds looked toward the east.[72] Le Petit adds that the eagles were painted red, yellow and white, and that the temple contained deities in human and animal forms.[73] James Adair also observed the figure of a large carved eagle on a pole at the apex of the roof of the winter hot house in the region.[74] It would be straining the imagination to prove a connection with the Horus falcon reaching the west[75] or surmounting the mast of Rameses III's ships but, viewed in the light of all the evidence presented in this book, the possibility should be entertained. Remember also that the Natchez temple had human deities in it and an eagle on the roof — so does this Egyptian shrine of c. 1250 B.C. (Fig. 123). The worship of deities here could itself be significant, for Garcilasso tells us that there were no idols or spell-making gods in the great Florida and the islands. 'They merely worship what Varro calls natural gods — the elements, the sea, lakes, rivers, springs, hills, wild animals, snakes,crops and similar things.'[76]

Figure 123

Add to this the fact that the solar ritual of the Natchez was closely paralleled by the Egyptian, as we shall see. Note first how the Timucua community of Florida used to worship the sun. The early contact drawing (Fig. 124) shows their chief, the priest and the others, raise both

Figure 124

arms toward the solar image,[77] in virtually the same manner as the high priest of Amun toward Re Harakhte in his solar boat (Fig . 125).[78]

Le Petit says about the Natchez that 'the sun is the principal object of veneration of the people... the great chief has the title "Brother of the Sun." ' The cabin on a mound on which he lives has his door fronting the east

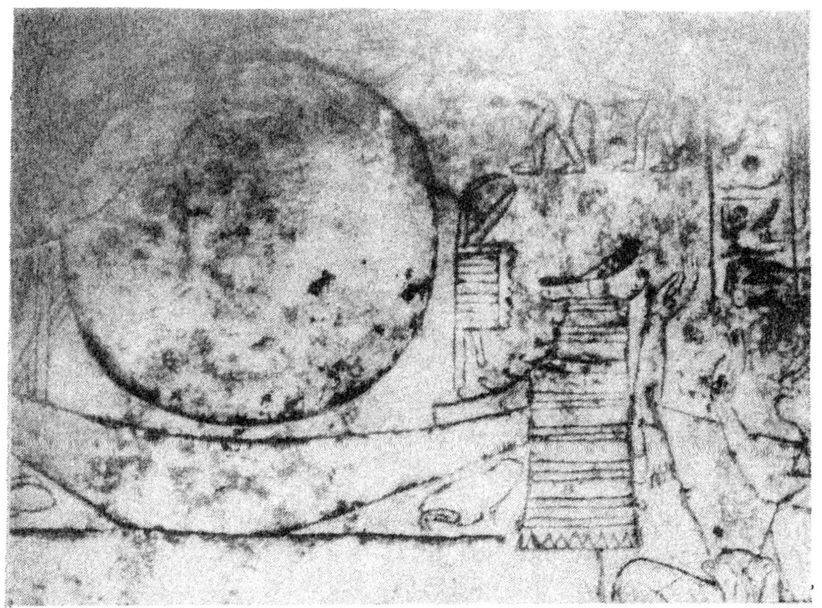

Figure 125

'and every morning the chief honours by his presence the rising of his older brother, and salutes him with many howlings as he appears above the horizon... afterward raising his hand above his head and turning from East to West he shows him the direction which he must take in his course.'[79] Both solar rituals are of Egyptian origin: the counterpart of the 'howling' is the 'shouting' at dawn by helpers of the sun described, for instance, in a text of Rameses III.[80] The directing of the sun from East to West is described in the text 'You shall go up on the great eastern side of the sky and go down on the great western side of the earth.'[81] A hymn to the sun praises Amon when he rises as Harakhte, as the great falcon bright of plumage.

Yet another conception in common survives in a different area, in Cherokee myth, in which the sun is held to enter by a door. The 'Journey to the Sunrise' relates[82] that a long time ago several young men made up their minds to find the place where the sun lives, and see what the sun is like. They got ready with their bows and arrows, their parched corn, and extra mocassins, and started out toward the East. At first they met ethnic groups they knew, then they came to communities they had only heard about, and at last to others of which they had never heard. They travelled on till at last they came to the sunrise place where the sky reaches down to the ground. Here there was a door — the sun came out of it from the East, and climbed along the inside of the arch. It had a human figure. Of the seven men, one was killed when he tried to enter the door. The others returned, but they had travelled so far that they were old when they reached home.

In addition to the 'Door by which the Sun enters,' which exists also in Egyptian mythology, there is a whole sequence of parallels between this Cherokee myth and the Ramessid journey to the West. The parallels are as follows:

1. The purpose of the journey was to find the place

where the sun sets in one case, and where it rises in the other.

2. Each is a deliberate expedition with an exploratory purpose.

3. Each assumes that the sky rests on the ends of the earth.

4. The sun in both cases has an anthropomorphic form.

5. There were seven expedition members in one case,

Figure 126

and seven expeditionary ships in the other.

The sequence of close parallels rules out coincidence.

Nor could it be coincidence that the Timucua queen of Florida was borne in procession (Fig. 126) on a litter with fan-bearers[83] much as was Rameses III (Fig. 127), long, long before.

Figure 127

Conclusion

These investigations into the overseas connections of the two areas of early North America have pointed to acommon source, yet we have arrived at very different solutions as to the degree and to the manner in which the transmissions may have been effected.

The great input of Egyptian civilization into Mexico could not have been accomplished by drift voyagers, but only by a considerable body of migrants with learned priests among them. They imposed their culture on the natives who were ready to learn more sophisticated ways than the simple agricultural mode of life to which they were accustomed. Through intermarriage and assimilation with the invaders, the native culture acquired a totally new complexion. In turn the peripheral areas of Mesoamerica felt the presence of the nuclear zone on the Gulf Coast, and responded to it in different ways. The diversity is explained by the fact that the whole land was not held together by imperial means,i.e., a centralised political system, and so had room to develop in relative freedom.

The lands to the north across the Gulf of Mexico beckoned, and at some early stage a bid was made to possess it. In the light of the evidence presented here it seems not to have succeeded, and the invaders were repelled by the fiercely independent American Indian communities who forged a temporary confederation and held out. The ceremonials and adopted traits are either the result of residues of the first invasion, or signs of fresh movements of traders drifting up from the South.

Postscript 1

(See chap. 1, pp.12-13)

Just before going to press, a very important piece of evidence, confirming my theory, came to my notice.

This illustration from a Mexican picture book from Coixtlahuaca (Fig.136), shows a man seated in a boat on top of a mountain with two peaks; *he is claimed to be the first ancestor.*[1] That this is no ordinary mountain is clear from the sacred (Yakshe) tree within it, whose roots stretch down into the Underworld. Remember, also, what Sahagun had said, that the first stage of the Underworld in Mexican belief was 'the place where the mountains came together.'[2] We had already seen, and I show again, the two-peaked mountain which was the entrance to the Underworld as shown in Seti 1's tomb (Fig.137).

Rameses 111 says, 'May I arrive safely...and mingle

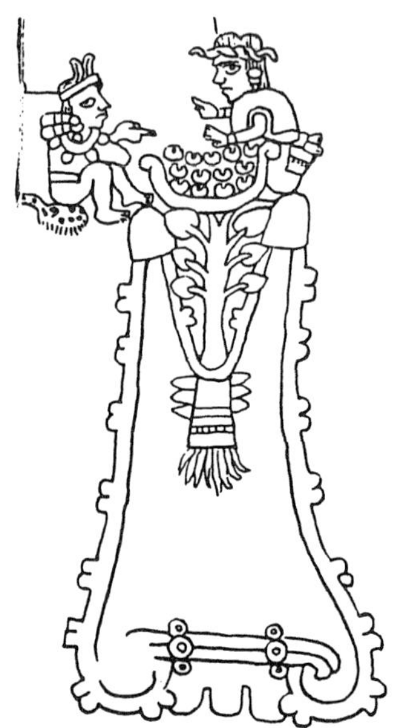

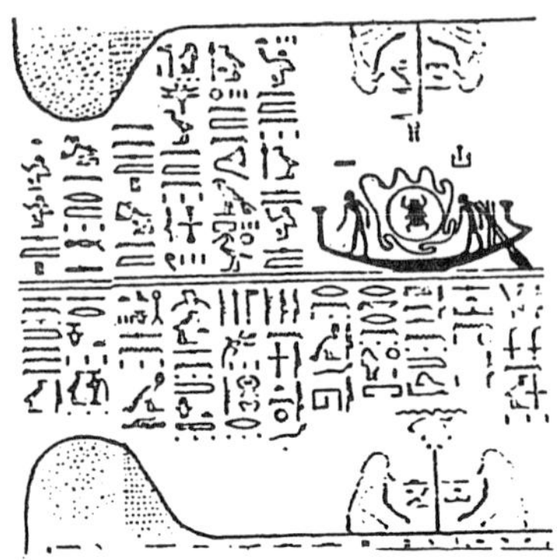

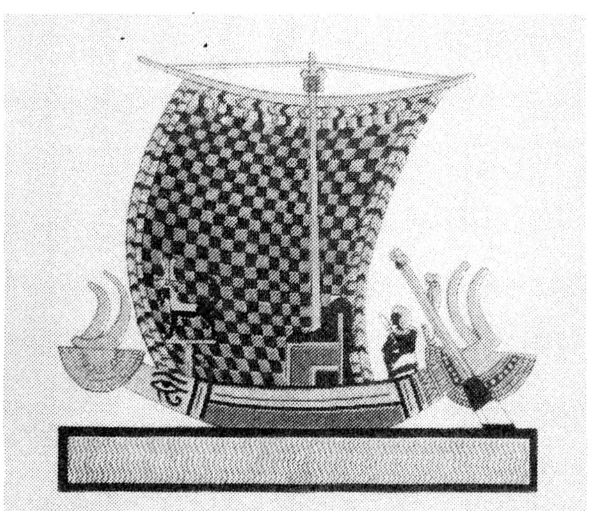

From left to right: Figures 136, 137, 138

with the excellent souls of Manu.[13] Notice the woman greeting the arrival in the boat; she is a native of the place with whom he will mingle. The identification of the person in the boat with Rameses 111 as shown in the solar boat in his tomb (Fig.138) is indicated by the fact that both figures are shown in profile, both are gesturing, and both are sitting in the stern of the boat (as the helmsman).

POSTSCRIPT 2

(See chap. 2, Ref.12)

On the latest discussion of transmission of cultigens to America, see T.J. Riley et al, in *Current Anthropology*, Vol. 31., No.5, December 1990.

(See Ref.51, ibid.)

Key Marco is an ancient marine shell island off the West Coast of Florida, 150 miles south of Tampa. The 100 wooden objects had been wonderfully preserved in the mangrove swamps. Among them was a wooden alligator whose jaws were hinged so that they could be snapped opened and shut (Frank H. Cushing, *Proceedings of the American Philosophical Society*, Vol. xxxv), recalling the wooden animals with movable jaws from Egyptian tombs, e.g., at the British Museum.

Appendix I

Symbolism of the Eagle Mound

(re. Fig. 122 above)

The closest relative of the eagle-form effigy mound at Poverty Point, Louisiana, is in Mexico. It is at the crucial Olmec site of San Lorenzo Tenochtitlan, which yielded so many of the Olmec heads, and much else of great interest. An aerial photograph shows, and the excavators admit, that 'the ancients had visualised some kind of gigantic animal effigy, a huge flying bird as seen from above.'[1]

Clearly there must be some implied symbolism, and in my view the key lies in a PreColumbian Mexican codex picture (Codex Madrid)[2] (Fig. 131). On the top right a black bird flies toward two stars of the night sky, one of which is nested in a minuscule boat. At the far left below is a skeletal figure with a glyph which helps to identify him as the god of the Underworld.[3]

Figure 131

Thus in effect the scenario is of a bird on its flight to the Underworld. It recalls the falcon rising from the horizon on an Egyptian 21st Dynasty sarcophagus.[4] In the Coffin Texts the falcon identifies itself: "I am the guide to the horizon of the sky"[5].

The person in the Mexican codex immediately below

the bird has his arms out stretched either receiving or donating a gift. The gift consists of a jar with a stack of three oval symbols resembling the Maya glyphs meaning 'maize'. Again their nearest equivalent is an Egyptian picture with three crosses-in-disks stacked on the bow of a boat cruising in the Underworld with the deceased (Fig. 132). The Egyptian glyph means 'the city', and its multiplication evidently implies the special city in the Underworld, the Seket Aaru. The adjacent scene shows

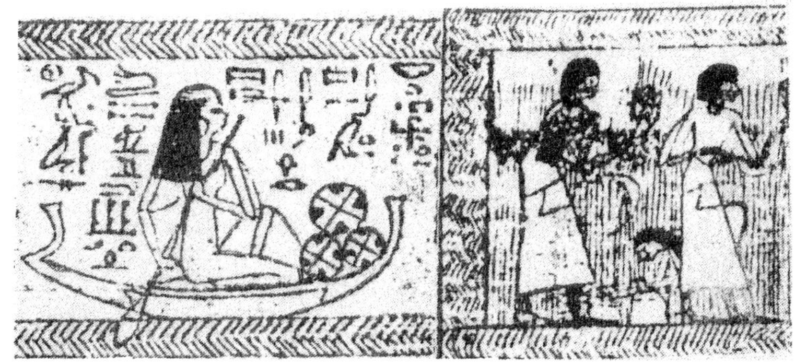

Figure 132

grain being harvested in the Underworld.

What then is the significance of the large fish's head which the Underworld god holds before him in the codex picture? It can scarcely be just the decapitated head of a fish, but symbolical like the rest of the scene. I contend that it is 'the Abtu fish that swims in the bow of the boat of the sun-god' which is mentioned in the Egyptian *Book of the Dead.* [6] To prove this, I turn to a relief from the site of Tejin, north of Veracruz on the Mexican Gulf.[7] It shows a priest, or surrogate for god, wearing a fish mask over his head. As in the Egyptian text, here too the sun-god is involved. He is shown above the shrine grasping a snake (Fig.133). He is

Figure 133

stretching it towards a person who is perfor-ming a pe-nance by perforating his penis with a spine. Elsewhere I had cited a text in which the Egyptian sun-god too per-forated his penis and draws blood.

Finally it should be observed that the fish-masked figure on the Tajin relief is shown in the choppy waters of the sea, as if he were literally like 'the Abtu fish at the prow of the sun's ship'. Working backwards from the Classical period into the Formative, we find the monumental fish once again, this time on an Olmec relief. It is over the head of the bearded Levantine with aquiline nose — evidently on the occasion of his marriage to the young

Figure 134

woman who stands before him (Fig. 134). The head-dress or crown is meaningless as the effigy of a real fish, but it is extremely significant if we accept its role as the pilot fish which guided the sun-god to this land (in its course from East to West), and the migrants too with it in a solar journey. The fish which appears next to the steering oars in a relief of the solar ship (see above Fig.125) is likely to be the Abtu fish.

To return to the theme of the eagle mound, I believe that both the mounds at San Lorenzo in Mexico and at Poverty Point in Louisiana were made in the form of solar eagles to signify that they had reached their destination in the West.* Thus the dwellers on the mounds could rest content that they had realized their goal and their mission.

---

*Note too above in Figure 71 where the eagle reaches its goal, and in Figure 87 where it presides over the mound.

Appendix 2

A Ramessid Temple in Peru

I drew up the parallels between Huaca de los Reyes in North Peru and Madinat Habu in Thebes in Egypt, (Figs. 134, 135) and sent them to Dr. Tom Pozorski of the Carnegie Museum of Natural History, Pittsburg, Pennsylvania, who had published the results of his excavations. He replied to me on May 7, 1982, and this is a summary of that correspondence.

He had suggested that Huaca de los Reyes had arisen out of earlier Peruvian edifices of the Initial Period. I replied that anyone who compared the two chief sites at Kotosh and El Paraiso would find none of the features I had pointed to. I admitted that there was an architectural tradition in Peru perhaps a thousand years in advance of any other place in the New World, but what I challenged was a demonstration of continuity between the structures of the Initial Period (after c.1800 B.C.) and the Formative Period (after c. 1200 B.C.). It was because there was a disjunction that origins had to be sought elsewhere.

Dr. Pozorski raised two further objections. First that the architectural materials in the two buildings I had compared were different, and second that the human figures at the two sites were different from each other. To this I replied that architectural materials are bound to be different in the two countries, reflecting as they do local traditions. And the human images cannot conceivably be identical since they appear to have been executed by native craftsmen under foreign instruction. The resemblance in the images, I claimed, are not in their visible form, but in the way they have been deployed: that is, there are in both cases consecutive human figures fronting each of the pillars along the side of the court — which is absolutely unique to the two parts of the world at the time in question. At Madinat Habu the figures are all of the founder Rameses III, and Dr. Pozorski had himself suggested in his thesis (1975/76, p. 178) that the standing figures in front of the pillars represented the same person — perhaps the founder or a more distant ancestor.

Dr. Pozorski's other objection that the layout in the two buildings is different is scarcely acceptable when the parallels are so precise, and when no other building of that date (both 12th century B.C.) in any part of the world has a remotely similar plan. I would go so far as to say that the architect who drew up the plan at Huaca de los Reyes must actually have been involved in the construction of Madinat Habu. Rameses III virtually confirms this when he makes the claim, made by no other Pharaoh, that the fame of his building had reached the ends of the earth.

On the following page I present the comparison in plan of the two edifices.

Key to parallels.

1. Successive courts laid out on a long axis.
2. Standing human figures carved in front of consecutive pillars.
3. Columns flanking court.
4. Staircase at junction of two courts.
5. Hypostyle hall across the axis beyond second court.
6. Tripartite division of space with equal parts and symmetry.
7. Axis culminates in a 4-pillared shrine.
8. Both buildings oriented to the West.

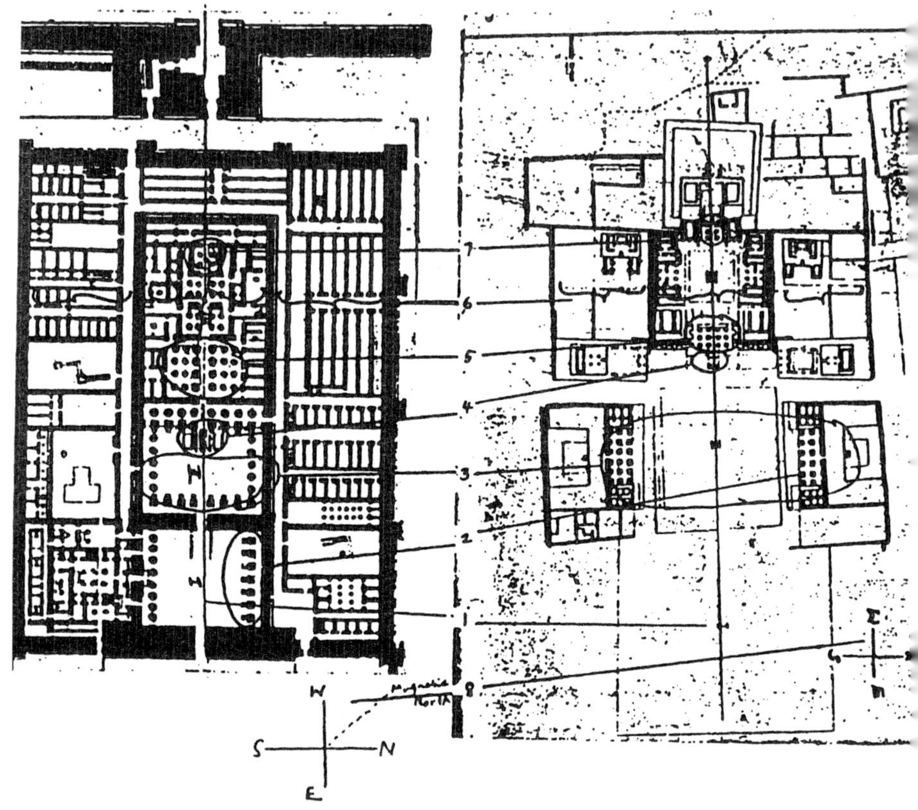

Figure 134: Madinat Habu, Egypt Figure 135: Huaca de Los Reyes, Peru

Postscript

My claim that Huaca de Los Reyes has no antecedents in Peru, now receives independent support (see J. Haas et al, *The Origins of the Andean State*, Cambridge, 1987. p.33).

Appendix 3

The Olmecs — Egyptians or Autochthonous?

When posterity stands judgement over the matter, Americanists will have to answer the charge of the sin of omission. Their omission is to turn a deliberate, blind eye to the possibility that the roots of America's first civilization, the Olmec, could lie somewhere outside the continent. The result of their refusal to look has left an empty void. Into this void have stepped the fantasy cults — the Atlantis mirages, and the extra-terrestrial hallucinations.

They thrive because just now public taste prefers science fiction to science fact. Americanists indirectly aid and abet this situation, for outlandish solutions can have no consequence, whereas cogent ones pointing to transcontinental origins could upset the applecart.

True, not all Americanists are of the same dye. Some among them burrow their heads in the sand and would rather not know. Others are timorous of stepping out of line and incurring the displeasure of their colleagues. Still others would heed only the guardians of authority, who they would like to think can do no wrong. And just a few plunge in and, regarding themselves as final arbiters, resort to denigration to achieve their ends. Such a one is the ex-politician Jacques Soustelle.[1] The succeeding analysis will show how far he succeeds.

1. Soustelle describes me as an *ultradiffusionist.* I disclaim this. An *ultra- or hyper-diffusionist* is one who believes in principle that all traits or ideas were transmitted across the entire globe, whether they can be proved or not.[2]

Compared with this, if any name-calling is necessary, I could be called a *conditional-diffusionist*. The condition is threefold: * there must be unique parallels in specific traits in two areas, and preferably no other; * there should be a narrow time-context serving as a link; and * there should be a basis for establishing the means of transmission. When all these criteria have been met, a degree of probability exists. And when further it is found that any single trait is accompanied by a host of others that point in the same direction, then the probability becomes a virtual certainty. And finally when it is found that there is nothing in the native or neighbouring environment to explain its nascence, then there is dead certainty (or as near as makes no difference). These are stringent conditions and, within the limits of human fallibility, must be met.

2. Soustelle says that by trying to prove too much, I prove nothing. This is strange arithmetic! I have always been led to believe that when you add one digit to another the sum total is advanced. The case I have presented is one of primary migration. Migrations do not bring merely single traits, but whole clusters. And who will gainsay that migrations have gone on throughout history and, from just one continent, have peopled the globe, though they had the most rudimentary means of transport? As far as the cluster goes, in this instance there were nuclei on both sides, and the imprints are indelible. In many cases the linear edges are sharp, and are like looking in a mirror; in others the edges have blurred, but still there is no mistaking the identity.

3. Soustelle says that I claim that practically all the peoples of Asia Minor and the Far East met on the shores of Mexico. This is gross exaggeration. First of all, Asia Minor is Turkey, and I have nothing whatever to say about this land. And of all the many Far Eastern nations,

I single out only the Chinese (in my book in question). As for the Africans and Levantines, there is nothing surprising in this, for if the Egyptians were there, the others would have been too, since they were enlisted in the Egyptian army and navy. As to his complaint that no Egyptians as such are discernible among the Olmecs, I would remind him that let alone a commoner, the Egyptian King himself is present on a painting in a Mexican pyramid (see above Fig.7). Nor is the Egyptian just any Pharaoh; it is Rameses III whose presence is felt countless times in Mexico, and who alone claims to have sent expeditions 'to the ends of the earth.' This picture (see above Fig. 3) is of him enjoying the delights of paradise, which in Egyptian belief, lies in the Underworld and whose entrance is situated in the Far West of the World. Mexican tradition as preserved by Sahagun confirms that the first ancestors who came to this land came looking for Paradise.[4] The motives are clear, and one account fortifies the other.

4. Soustelle asks: 'Can we believe that if the Egyptians were in Mexico they would not have left a single hieroglyph?' He ignores the two Egyptian hieroglyphs in Mexico I had pointed to then,[5] and to these I had added two more in 1981.[6] It is only a question of time before more will be found or identified, even though Olmec excavations have either been restricted or curtailed over the past decade for suspect reasons. Soustelle further

glosses over the testimony of Sahagun, which I had cited, and in which he says that the first ancestors who had come across the seas brought their *books* with them, and when they decided to go away in their search, they took their books with them, and others who remained had to reinvent the calendar and glyphs.[7] A vague allusion is made to this by Soustelle in a cynical manner, but the reader is told nothing of this to enable one to form one's own judgement.

5. Soustelle says that the parallels I point to are too general. Many of them are, on the contrary, incredibly exact. He chooses monarchy as an example. I do not claim to prove that monarchy as such was transmitted, but only the paraphernalia associated with it. In my second volume published in 1976,[8] I listed the following specific details of Pharaonic kingship to be found in Olmec or later Mexico:

* the tail, * the double crown, * the parasol, * the flail, * and the coronation ritual of shooting arrows to the four cardinal directions. Similarly, in every area of life, death, and thought, I point to precise not 'general resemblances,' and in most cases *unique* to the two areas concerned.

6. Soustelle refers to my erroneous interpretations of facts observed, and gives as an example the cylindrical object held in the hand of an Olmec statue. He denies that it is an Egyptian scroll. I had pointed this out

cautiously as a possibility, since the person is seated like an Egyptian scribe. The politician Soustelle said this in his French edition in 1979, but unfortunately for him, the archaeologists Coe and Diehl agree with me in 1980 that 'the figure which bears an uncanny resemblance to the scribal effigy of ancient Egypt, is seated tailor-fashion. He grasps a bar or scroll across his knees'[9] which is just what Egyptian scribes did. The Olmec scroll has the same general proportions of that in the lap of the Egyptian scribe. Like the scroll shown, it is likely to have been the *Book of the Dead*', whose presence I have detected in numerous occasions in Mexico,[10] and which was, after all, their "passport to eternity," and consequently would have to have been there.

7. According to Soustelle, I am jumbling together facts from different cultures of Mexico, and this can't be done because they were quite distinct civilizations. First of all, whenever possible I am drawing my material from Olmec artifacts, but if I do step outside that culture I say so clearly since the Olmec phenomena were but recently found and in the words of Ignacio Bernal, 'the immense majority of the sites are still to be explored.'[11] But he himself admits that 'we are dealing with one civilization only because of its common basis, both branches (Aztec and Maya) have parallel history as well as innumerable points of contact.'[12]

Soustelle's second collaborator Coe too speaks of the

unity and continuity of 'this great religious system, apparently founded by the Olmecs.'[13] And indeed Soustelle himself resorts to double standards by admitting the continuity of Olmec motifs and civilization for 2000 years in one place, and 3000 years in another.[14] So if there is any "jumbling," it was one of history, and not of my contrivance.

8. Soustelle asks: 'Why would these voyagers, once settled in Mexico, have taken the trouble to perpetuate in stone, at the cost of tremendous physical effort the faces of the 'Ethiopian slaves' rather than their own countenances?' It is likely that the greatest majority of the sailors were of Nubian stock, and among them were some who would have held positions of authority, as we in fact know in other instances. Nubians were actually involved in a conspiracy against Rameses III,[15] but whereas this was foiled at home, it could have succeeded abroad (as suggested by the decapitated head of the scribe). A second explanation as to why the Olmecs carved heads is that Nubian heads were then being carved in Egypt and only in Egypt, and moreover I have just discovered that those who quarried stones and transported them by river in Rameses III's time were actually called "heads!."[16]

At any rate, what is even more important, is that colossal sculpture on the scale of the Olmec heads was being produced nowhere but in Egypt at the time, and subsequently in Assyria. The Greeks learned to carve human statues from the Egyptians in the 7th century B.C., and the Indians from the Greeks in the 2nd century B.C.[17], so there is nothing unusual about this pattern recurring yet earlier in Mexico (12th century B.C.). In a protracted work on sculpture published in 1986, Parsons comes to the conclusion that 'Antecedents for Olmec stone sculpture have not been found... I now believe they never will be found in Mesoamerica.'[18]

9 And finally, let it be noted that carping is one thing, but fiddling with the figures is another. Soustelle says that I am pointing to Egyptian evidences from the middle of the 3rd millennium B.C. I am not — I am citing all but a few from the time of Rameses III (1198 - 1167 B.C.). In my three-volume work, *The Origins of American Civilisation,* this King appears in 117 different contexts with reference to the Americas.[19] And I repeat, *he is the only Pharaoh to claim that he built a feet and sent it to the ends of the earth, and it is precisely in his reign that Olmec civilization appeared in Mexico.*

Conclusion

Soustelle dubbed me an *ultra-diffusionist* which I have shown to be inaccurate, but he himself is an *arch-*

Isolationist which he will not be able to deny. He has the temerity to call Olmec civilization "autochthonous" (p. 194). As we have seen, he has attempted to do this with weak and fallacious reasoning. What his motives are one can guess but need not rake up. Be this as it may, it has nothing to do with saving Mexico from embarrassment. As Green says: 'No culture was truly *sui generis* as none existed in total isolation.'[20] The Mexicans are in good company with the best. They need no longer feel that they are out on a limb, cut off from their equals in the Old World. They must be glad to have learned that they are heirs to a rich and famous ancestry, and further to be aware that they began with this inheritance and went on to utterly transform it to reflect their own natural genius.

REFERENCES

Chapter 1

Note: The chief sources of this chapter appear in previous works of this author as follow:

Ancient Egyptians and Chinese in America, 1974.
Asians in PreColumbian Mexico, 1976.
Ancient Egyptians in Middle and South America, 1981.
"Further evidences of Egyptian intrusion in PreColumbian Mexico", *The New Diffusionist,* Bedfordshire, No.18, Jan. 1975, p.8f.

1. Breasted, J.H., *Ancient Records of Egypt,* Chicago, 1906-7, IV, pp.140, 60-
2. Sahagun, *Florentine Codex, General History of the things of New Spain,* tr. A.J.O Anderson & C.E. Dibble, Santa Fe, New Mexico, 1950-63, Bk6, pp.162-3.
3. *Popol Vuh,* tr. Edmonson, *The Book of Council: The Popol Vuh of the Quiche Maya of Guatemala,* New Orleans, 1971, 6057f.
4. Pritchard, J.B., ed., *Ancient Near Eastern Texts,* Princeton, 1955, p. 448.
5. Sahagun, ibid, Bk.10, p.191.
6. *Popol Vuh,* 1971, 7240f.
7. Nicholson, I., *Mexican and Central American Mythology,* London, 1968, p.22; Frankfort, H., *Kingship and the Gods,* Chicago, 1948, p.79f.; Fairman, H.W., in Hooke, S.H., ed., *Myth, Ritual, and Kingship,* 1958, pp.83-4.
8. Carmack, R.M., *Quichean Civilisation,* Berkeley, 1973, p.294.
9. Edgerton, W.F., & Wilson, J.A., *Historical Records of Rameses III,*

Chicago, 1936, pp.120-1.

10. Reichel-Dolmatoff, G., "The feline motif in Prehistoric San Augustin Sculpture," in E.P. Benson, ed., *Cult of the Feline*, Dum-barton Oaks, Washington D.C., 1972, pp.51-68.
11. Garcilasso, *The Royal Commentary of the Incas,* tr. M. Jolas, London, 1963, p.369, cf. p.15.
12. Edgerton, W.F. & Wilson, J.A., op. cit., 1936, pp.13-14.
13. Bancroft, H.H., *Native Races,* San Francisco, 1883, II, pp.603-4.
14. Zuidema, "Meaning in Nazca Art", *Goteborg Etnografiken Museum,* Arstryck, 1971, pp.35-54.
15. Pritchard, J.B., *op. cit.,* 1955, p.260; Breasted, J.H., 1906-7, IV, p.203.
16. Edgerton, W.F. & Wilson, J.A. op. cit., 1936, p.148, cf. p.152.
17. Mercer, S.A.B., *The Pyramid Texts,* 1952, New York, London, I, pp.90, 165.
18. Lefebure, M.E., *Les Hypogées Royaux de Thèbes,* (Annales de Musée Guimet, Vol.16), 1889, pp.91-2; Champollion, *Monuments de l'Egypte et de la Nubie,* new ed. Paris, 1945, III, pl. CCLVI; Rosellini, J., *Monumenti dell Egitto e della Nubia,* Pisa, 1832-44, II, pls.107, 108.
19. Sahagun, *Historia de las Cosas de Nueva Espana,* Mexico, 1946, pp.13-14; Sorenson, J.L., "Some Mesoamerican traditions of immigration by sea," *El Mexico Antiguo,* Mexico, Dec. 1955, VIII, p.429.
20. Budge, E.A.W., *The Egyptian Heaven and Hell,* 1906, London, I, pp.47-8.

20a. Schoff, H.W., ed., *The Periplus of the Erythraean Sea,* London, etc.,

21. *Popol Vuh,* op. cit, 1971, 5921-2.
22. Herodotus, II, 49. See further on this subject, R.A. Jairazbhoy, op, cit, 1974, pp.46-48.
23. Naville, E., *Temple of Deir al Bahri,* 1901, IV, pl.C; and de Vries, C.E., "A ritual ballgame", *Studies in honour of John A Wilson,* 1969, pp. 25-35.
24. Blackman, A.M., "The significance of Insence and Libations," *Zeitschrift fur agyptische Sprache und Altertumskunde,* Berlin Bd.50; Elliot Smith, G., *The Migrations of Early Culture,* Manchester, 1929, p.42.
25. Popol Vuh, *op. cit.,* 1971, 6249-6255; Budge, E.A.W., *Egyptian Magic,* 1901, pp. 192, 195.
26. Budge, E.A.W., *The Book of the Dead,* (British Museum Guide), London, 1929, p.23; Sahagun, op. cit, Bk.I, pp.8,9.
27. Sahagun, op. cit., 1950-63, Bk.10, p.190.
28. Boylan, P., *Thoth the Hermes of Egypt,* London, 1922, p.58.
29. Sahagun, op. cit., 1950-63, Bk.2, 32; illus.89.
30. Frye, R.N., "Gestures of deference to royalty in Ancient Iran,", *Iranica*

Antiqua, Leiden, IX, 1972, pp.102-107, esp. p. 104.
31. See Jairazbhoy, R.A., op. cit., 1974, pp.23-24.
32. Pritchard, J.B., op. cit., 1955, p. 261.
33. Wiercinski, A., "Ricerca antropologia sugli olmechi", *Terra Ameriga,* Nos.18-19, Rapallo. See also Juan Comas, *Anales de Antropologia,* VIII, Mexico, 1971, pp.302-4.
34. Save-Soderbergh, T., *The navy of the 18th Egyptian Dynasty,* Uppsala, Leipzig, 1946.
34a. Breasted, J., *Ancient Records of Egypt,* III, 290.
34b. Ibid, IV, p.203.
35. Clark, R.T.R., *Myth and Symbol in Ancient Egypt,* London, 1959, p.56; and Naville, E., op. cit., 1901, pt.4, pl.CXV.
36. Sahagun, op. cit., Bk.2, 77.
37. Budge, E.A.W., *The Book of the Dead,* London, 1969, p.266 (Ch. LXXXII, 3).
38. Ibid., 1969, p.154, (ch.XXVI, 7).
39. Sahagun, op. cit., 1969, Bk. 6, pp.162, 164; cf. Daressy, G., *Notice explicative des ruines de Medinet Habu,* Cairo, 1897, pp.159-160; and *Popol Vuh,* op.cit., 1971, 5937-9, 6039.
40. Clark, R.T.R., op.cit., 1959, p.85.
41. Mercer, S.A.B., *Horus, Royal God of Egypt,* Grafton, Mass., 1942, p.130.
42. Caso, A., *The Aztecs, People of the Sun,* 1967, pp.32-33; and Sahagun, op.cit, 1969, Bk. 6, p.32.
43 Clark, R.T.R., op.cit.., 1959, p.216.
44. Sahagun, op.cit., 1950-69, Bk.6 , p.163.
45. Sahagun, ibid, p.239; Breasted, J.H., op cit., 1906-7, IV, p.115.
46. Edgerton, W.F., & Wilson, J.A., 1936, op.cit., pp.38, 42, 57,
47. Pritchard, J.B., op.cit., 1955, p.12.
48. Breasted, J.H., op.cit., 1906-07, IV, p.203.
49. Montet, P., *Everyday Life in Egypt,* 1958, p.298.
50. Budge, E.A.W., op. cit., 1906, III, p.153.
51. Budge, E.A.W., *The Gods of the Egyptians,* 1904, I, p.204.
52. Budge, E.A.W.., ibid, 1904, I, pp.257-8; 1906, op. cit.,I, p.259; Piankoff, A., *The Shrines of Tut-Ankh-Amon,* New York, 1955, p.94; Clark, R.T.R., op.cit., pp.209-10. For detailed comparisons see Jairazbhoy, R.A., op.cit., 1974, pp.73-5.
53. Sahagun, *Historia de las Cosas de Nueva Espana,* Mexico, 1880, pp.587-9.
54. *Popol Vuh,* op.cit., 1971, 1,.5063-6, 5700f.

55. Sahagun, op.cit, 1950-69, Bk.3, p.41; cf. Budge, E.A.W., op.cit., 1929, p.13.
56. Heizer, R.F., "The La Venta fluted pyramid", *Antiquity*, 42, 1968, pp. 52-6; cf. Davies, N. de, *Two Ramesside Tombs at Thebes,* New York, 1927, p.98, pls. xiii, xiv.
57. For detailed comparisons and texts, see Jairazbhoy, R.A., op. cit., 1974, pp.69-71.
58. Jairazbhoy, R.A., op. cit.,1974, pp.67, 83-4, 71-2.
59. Birch, S., *Egyptian Texts of the earliest period from the Coffin of Amanu in the British Museum,* London, 1886, p.14.
60. Tozzer, A. M., tr., *Landa's Relacion de las Cosas de Yucatan,* Peabody Museum, 1941, p.131.
61. Zabkar, L.V., *A study of the Ba concept in Ancient Egyptian Texts,* 1968, p.140. Notice the great bird on top of the tree at Palenque. It is paralleled by the *smen* goose alighting on the beautiful sycamore tree (Budge, E.A.W., op. cit., 1969, p. 640 (ch. CLXXXIX, 11).
62. *Popol Vuh,* op. cit., 1971, 7154; cf. Piankoff, A., "The Sky-goddess Nut and the Night Journey of the Sun," *Journal of Egyptian Archaeology,* XX, 1934, p.59.
63 Zabkar, L.V., op. cit., 1968, p.131.
64. Budge, E.A.W., op. cit., 1969, pp.631, 658-9; and Budge, E.A.W., 1913, p.414.

Chapter 2

1 Holmes, Wm. H., in *Science,* April 11, 1884.
2. Holmes, Wm. H., 'Bells' in *Handbook of American Indians*, Bureau of American Ethnology, Bulletin 30, Pt. 1, Washington, 1907, p. 141.
3. Nuttal, Z., in Moorehead, W, K, *Etowah Papers*, 1932 p. 144, fig. 57d.
4. Krieger, A. D., "Recent developments in the problem of relationships between the Mexican Gulf Coast and Eastern United States", in *Huastecas, Totonacos, y sus recinos,* ed. I. Bernal and E. Davalos, Mexico, 1953, pp. 497 - 518.
5. Willey, G.,. *An Introduction of American Archaeology,* I, 1966, p. 305.

6. Griffin, J. B., "Mesoamerica and the Eastern United States in Prehistoric times", *Handbook of Middle American Indians,* ed. Wauchope, R., Austin, Texas, IV, 1965, p. 118.
7. *Ibid,* 1965, pp. 119 - 120.
8. *Op. cit.*, I, 1966, p. 522.
9. Ford, U. A., *A Comparison of Formative Cultures in the Americas,* Washington, 1969, p. 193.
10. Marshall, J.: "American Indian Geometry", *Ohio Archaeologist,* 28, 1978, 1, pp. 29 - 33; cf. Griffin, J. B., in *Hopewell, ed., Archaeology,* Kent, Ohio, 1979, p. 277 — who expresses scepticism.
11. Struever, S. and Vickery, K. D.: "The beginning of cultivation in the Midwest-Riverine area of the United States", *American Anthropologist,* 75, 1973, pp. 1197 - 1220.
12. Griffin, J. B. op. cit., 1965, p. 119.
13. Ibid, 1965, p. 128.
14. Ibid, 1965, p. 124.
15. Ibid, 1965, p. 127f
16. Porter, M. N., *Pipas Pre Cortesianas,* Acta Anthropologica, 3, 2, 1948.
17. See Jairazbhoy, R. A., *Ancient Egyptians and Chinese in America,* London, 1974; and *Ancient Egyptians in Middle and South America,*1981.
18. Moore, C. B., "Moundville revisited", *Journal of the Academy of Natural Sciences of Philadelphia,* vol. 13, pt. 3, 1907, pp. 337 - 405; pl. XXXIIIa
19. Gay, C. T. E., *Chalcacingo, 1971,* pp. 56, 59; Grove, D. C., Chalcatzingo, 1984, p. 112.
20. Cooper, W. R., *The Serpent myths of Ancient Egypt,* London, 1873, fig. 102, p. 61.
21 Ibid, 1873, fig. 19, p. 12.
22. Papyrus of Padiu-Khons, 21st Dynasty, British Museum no. 10004.
23. Hart, G. *A Dictionary of Egyptian Gods and Goddesses,* 1986, p. 203.
24. Spinden, H. J., *Maya Art and Civilisation,* 1957, pp.238 — 9, p. 243f.
25. Morgan, W. N., *Prehistoric Architecture in the Eastern United States,* Cambridge, Mass., 1980.
26. *Handbook of American Indians North of Mexico,* I, 1907, p. 444.
27. Cf. Moorehead, W. K., ed., *Etowah Papers,* New Haven, 1932, Fig. 14.
28. Hamilton, H. W., *Spiro Mound Copper,* (Memoir of the Missouri Archaeological Society, No. 11), 1974, pp. 74 - 6.
29. See *American Antiquity,* Vol. 36, No. 1, 1971, p. 99, fig. 3.
30. Murray, Margaret, "Ritual masking", *Melanges Maspero,* Le Caire,1934, I fasc. 1, p. 254.

31. Champollion, *Monuments de l 'Egypte, et de la Nubie*, Vol. III, Paris, 1845, pl. CCXII.
32. Cf. F. J. Dockstader, *Indian Art in America*, New York,1973, pl. 64; drawing by C. Hudson, *Elements of S.E. Indian Religion*, Leiden, 1984, pl. XXIIIa.
33. *Etowah Papers*, ed. Moorehead, W. K. , New Haven,1932, fig. 13.
34. Cf. Touny, A. D. and Wenig, S., *Der Sport in Alten Agypten*, Leipzig, 1969, pls. 15 - 18.
35. *Madinat Habu*, Oriental Institute of Chicago, pl. 35.
36. Hellmuth, N. M., *PreColumbian Ballgame* (Foundation for Latin American Anthropological Research, Progress Report), Guatemala City, Vol. I, no. 1, March 1975, p. 8.
37. Diego Duran, II, 244.
38. Williams, Stephen,ed., *The Waring Papers*, (Papers of the Peabody Museum of Archaeology and Ethnology, LVIII, 1968), Cambridge, Mass., p. 56.
39. Cf. Andrews, G. F., *Maya Cities*, Norman, Oklahoma, 1975, Fig. 290.
40. *The Waring Papers, op. cit.*, 1968, p. 14, Fig. 4b.
41. Holmes, W. H., "Art in shell of Ancient Americans', *Second Annual Report of the Bureau of American Ethnology*, Washington, D. C., 1883, opp. p. 288.
42. Adams, R. E. W., ed. *The origins of Maya civilisation*,
43. Drucker, P., *La Venta, Tabasco*, Smithsonian Institution Bureau of American Ethnology, Bulletin, 153, 1952, p. 170. 1974, pp. 207 - 8.
44. Caso, A., in *Handbook of Archaeology in Southern Mesoamerica*, 1965, p. 932, Fig. 1b.
45. Joralemon, P. D., *A study of Olmec Iconography*, Dumbarton Oaks, Washington, D. C., 1971, pp. 56 - 7.
46. Hudson, C., *Elements of Southern Indian Religion*, Leiden, 1974, pl. XXXVI. (photo, author).
47. Chapman, J., *American Indians in Tennessee, an archaeological perspective*, Knoxville, 1982, front.
48. Burland, C. *North American Indian Mythology*, Museum of Primitive Art, New York, 1965, p. 121.
49. Griffin, J. B., ed. *Archaeology of the Eastern United States*, 1952, Fig. 108 D., p. 196.
50. Jairazbhoy, R. A., *Ancient Egyptians in Middle and South America*, 1981, pp. 3 - 4.
51. Gilliland, M. S., *The material culture of Key Marco, Florida*, Gainsville, 1975; Hudson, C., *op. cit.*, pl.XXVIIIa
52. Cf. de la Fuente, B., *Escultura huasteca en piedra*, Mexico, 1980, pls.

CCVIIf.
53. Pritchard, J. B., ed. *Ancient Near Eastern Texts,* Princeton, 1955, p. 247.
54. British Museum, *Guide to the Fourth, Fifth and Sixth Rooms*, London, 1922, pp. 175 - 6.
55. Edgerton, W. F., and Wilson, J. A., *Historical Records of Rameses III,* Chicago, 1936, p. 80.
56. Cushing, Frank H., "Exploration of Ancient Key dweller's remains on the Gulf of Florida",*APS. P.,* 35 1897, 153, pp. 329 - 432, pl. XXXV.
57. William, Bartram, *Observations on the Creek and Cherokee Indians, 1789*, American Ethnological Society, Transactions Vol. 3, pt. 1, 1853, p. 18.
58. Jairazbhoy, R. A., *op. cit.*, 1974, part 6, 'Egyptian gods in Mexico' and *op. cit.*, 1981, pp. 14 - 19.
59. Meredith, H. L. and Milam, V. E., ed. *A Cherokee Vision of Eloh*, tr. Proctor, W., Bacone College, 1981.
60. *The Waring Papers*, *op. cit.*, 1968, p. 47.
61. Cf. Henige, D. P., *The Chronology of Oral tradition,* Oxford, 1974; p. 5.
61a. G. Hart, *A Dictionary of Egyptian Gods and Goddesses*, 1986, p.188.
62. Sears, W. H., "Seaborne contacts between the early cultures in the Lower S. E. United States and Middle through S. America", *The Sea in the PreColumbian World,* ed. Benson, E. P., Washington, 1977, pp. 1 - 13, Fig. 3 - `photo Florida AtlanticUniversity, Boca Raton.
63. See Drucker, P., *La Venta, Tabasco,*Smithsonian Institution Bureau of American Ethnology, Bulletin 153, p. 183. (upper portion).
64. Sears, W. H., *op. cit.,* 1977, p. 11.
65. Ford, J. A., *A Comparison of Formative Cultures in the Americas,* Smithsonian Contributions to Anthropology, Vol. II, Washington, 1969, p. 191.
65a. C. Webb, *The Poverty Point Culture,* Baton Rouge,Louisiana, 2nd ed. 1982
66. Ford, J.A. 1969, pp. 45 - 6.
67. Jairazbhoy, R. A., op. cit., 1974, p 66.
68. Breasted, J, H., *Ancient Records of Egypt*, Chicago,1906 - 07, IV, p. 25. For 'Great Circle' see also *Pyramid Texts,*Mercer, S. A. B., p. 125.
69. Webb, C. H., "The extent and content of Poverty Point Culture", *American Antiquity,* July 1965, Vol. 33, no. 3, 1968.
70. Gatschet A. S., *A migration legend of the Creek Indians*, I, 1884, pp. 222 -3.
71. Ibid, 1884, p. 120.
72. Neitzal, R. S., *Archaeology of the Feltham landsite, the grand village of the Natchez,* Antropological papers of American Museum of Natural History,

Vol. 51 pt. 1, New York, 1965, p. 70.
73. Ibid, 1965, p. 71. See also Swanton J. R., *Indian Tribes of the Lower Mississippi Valley*, Bureau of American Ethnology, no. 43, 1911.
74. Adair, J., *History of the American Indians,* 1875, pp30, 419.
75. Jairazbhoy, R. A., *op. cit.*, 1974, pp. 66, 113.
76. Garcilaso de la Vega, *Royal Commentaries of the Incas*, tr. H. V. Livermore, 1966, Austin, p. 83. (citing Blas Valera).
77. Engraving by de Bry after a drawing by Le Mayne who visited Florida in 1564/5. cf. Swanton, J. R., *op.cit.*, 1911, p. 102.
78. Dates from c. 890 B. C. British Museum EA 1224.
79. Swanton, J. R.., *op. cit.*, 1911, p. 102.
80. Jairazbhoy, R. A., *op. cit.*, 1974, p. 75. See now also Jairazbhoy, *Ancient Egyptian Survivals in the Pacific,* London, Karnak House, 1990.
81. Karenga, M., *Selections from the Husia*, L.A., University of Sankore Press, 1984, p.114.
82. Mooney, J., *Myth of the Cherokees*, Washington, 1902, p. 256.
83. Fundaburk, *Suncircles and Human Hands,* 1957, pls. 62, 160

Appendix I

1. Coe, M. and Diehl, R. A., *In the land of the Olmec,* 1980, I, pp. 26 28.
2. Anders, F., *Codex Tro-Cortesianus,* museo de America, Madrid, 1967, pl. 34.
3. Cf. Fig. 78 above.
4. Goff, B. L., *Symbols of Ancient Egypt in the Late Period,* 1979, p. 101.
5. Faulkener, R. O., 1973, p. 206. In view of the cross-in-disk in the Mexican codex in front of the god of the Underworld, it is remarkable that a *Coffin Text* says 'May you come to the great city... May you come before Osiris' (i.e. god of the Underworld). (Faulkener, R. O., 1975, p. 2)
6. Budge, EA. W., *The Book of the Dead,* 1969, Introductory Hymn, p.6.
7 Kampen, M. E, *The Sculptures of El Tajin*, Gainsville 1972, Fig. 24.

Appendix 3

1. J. Soustelle, *The Olmecs, the oldest civilisation in Mexico,* Norman, Oklahoma, 1985, pp. 28, 191. See also my analysis of a critique by another ex-politician Nigel Davies, *Voyages to the New World, fact or fantasy,* 1979; reviewed in *Historical Diffusionism,* 27, 1979, pp. 37 - 42
2. On this question see *The Concepts of Human Evolution* (Elliot Smith Centenary), ed. Lord Zucherman, London, 1973, p. 441f.
3. R. A Jairazbhoy, *Asians in PreColumbian Mexico,* London, 1976, plates 53, 54.
4. R. A. Jairazbhoy, *ancient Egyptians and Chinese in America,* London, 1974, p. 8.
5. *Ibid,* 1974, p. 39.
6. R. A. Jairazbhoy, *Ancient Egyptians in Middle and South America,* London, 1981, p. 76.
7. *Op. cit.,* 1974, p. 39.
8. *Op. cit.,* 1976, pp. 104, 105 and notes 21, 22, 23.
9 M. D. Coe and R. Diehl, *In the Land of the Olmec,* Austin, London, 1980, I, p. 317.
10. R. A Jairazbhoy *op. cit.,* 1981, e.g. pp. 93, 94 and throughout *op. cit.* 1974.
11. Ignacio Bernal, *The Olmec World,* Berkeley, 1976, p. 2.
12. *Ibid,* 1976, p. 7.
13. M. D. Coe, *In the Iconography of Middle American Sculpture,* ed. Metropolitan Museum of Art, 1973, p.10.
14. J. Soustelle, *op. cit., 1985, pp. 50, 194.*
15. See G. Steindorf and K. C. Seele, *When Egypt ruled the East,* 1965, pp. 255 - 6.
16. I shall publish this reference shortly in a forthcoming work.
17. R. A. Jairazbhoy, *The Spread of Ancient Civilisations,* Ra Publication (c/o the present author), 1982, pp. 104 - 6, and 167 - 8.
18. L. A. Parsons, *The Origins of Maya Art,* Dumbarton Oaks, Washington DC., 1986, p. 88.
19 R. A. Jairazbohy, *op. cit.,* 1981, pp. 89 - 90.
20. A. R. W. Green, *The role of human sacrifice in the Ancient Near East,* Missola, Montana, 1975, p. 202.

Postscript to Chapter 2

1. R. Parmenter, *Four Lienzos of the Coixtlahuaca Valley*, Washington D.C., Dumbarton Oaks, 1982, p.64. Fig.34. Reproduced with kind permission.
2. Sahagun, *Florentine Codex*, Book 3, Appendix, Chap.2.
3. Breasted. J.H., *Ancient Records of Egypt*, USA, Vol.IV, 1906-7, pp.140, 160-2.